Exhortation to my Dear Sister

To the girl who still has a chance at a clean slate

Pontso Phakoe

© Pontso Phakoe 2018

Exhortation to my dear sister

Published by Pontso Phakoe@Litpathways
Alberton, South Africa
litpathways@gmail.com

ISBN 978-0-620-81399-0

2 4 6 8 10 9 7 5 3 1

All rights reserved. No part of this publication may be reproduced, stored in a retrieval system, or transmitted in any form by any means electronic, mechanical, photocopying, recording or otherwise without the written permission of the copyright owner.

Layout and cover design by Boutique Books
Printed in South Africa by Digital Action

Poko, Hlompho le Khanya li isoe ho Uena Molimo

For my father, the Rev RT Phakoe:

"The hymns are sung, the prayers are lifted up, the sermons are preached"

Contents

Foreword by Rev B Phakoe	7
Defining the Problem	13
Birthright	23
Knowing God, Knowing Yourself	43
Hidden Treasure	57
Eyes of the Father	75
Self-correction	87
A Clean Slate	107
Love	133
Stepping Out	157
Living, Not Surviving	169
Today Informs Tomorrow	193

Foreword by Rev B Phakoe

*I*T WAS ON THE 10TH of February 2018 when she told me: "I am writing a book". I am not sure if it was before I responded or in the same breath that she also said: "I wrote one page. Pray with me, that His will be done".

It has been the story of our life. My sister's life has always been characterised by "a series of taking one step at a time" and all I've ever done has always been to pray for her. "May you be blessed, my sister! You shall do great things and also still prevail". This was in the spirit and manner that Saul blessed David; and indeed grace upon grace she saw. I thank God for the sister He gave me; and for the blessing she has become.

I thank God for the guidance we had as we grew up. At the time we did not value or cherish it, but in hindsight we were blessed to be placed in the family we had, which moulded and modelled us into the people we are; not perfect, but by the grace of God we are. We can say, like Paul, that His grace toward me was not in vain.

As you have the gift of "youth", regardless of your circumstances, please read this book and you will never regret it. Though this book is aimed at young girls, it can also guide young boys to being men of valour, who have respect for women and have a great walk with God. If you read this book, you will never live in regret that "youth is wasted on the young", for today informs tomorrow.

I am confident that these exhortations can change a life.

May you be blessed in the name of the Father, the Son and the Holy Spirit.

Bohlale Phakoe

Dear Sis,

I am writing this memo as a big sister to a younger sister: it is from my heart to yours. It is intentionally a simple memo to help you navigate life in Southern Africa as a young black female working towards not being labelled as *disadvantaged, impoverished* or any other word used when you are born on a continent known for its darkness rather than its light.

Most young black South African girls are being raised by women who were set free just a moment ago, at the official ending of apartheid. These women are themselves still trying to understand what being emancipated means. Most young black girls in all of Southern Africa are raised up by women who are still ruled by unjust systems including patriarchy, poverty, racial prejudice, being uneducated and the like. It is only recently that women have had the liberty to attempt to walk in their full emancipation. We are told that we have every right in the world that other modern people have, but this is difficult to believe because most doors are still closed by money we still don't have and qualifications we've only recently attained, while the key to opening the doors is "experience".

I am trained as a gynaecologist and a preacher of the Word of God, and I am tired of seeing the same problems that young ladies go through over and over again – and, each time, everyone seems to travail in isolation and each one of us thinks that we are the first human being to have such problems.

In this memo I try in the first instance to list a present day problem. Often you will find yourself in some of these dynamics and, in the same breath, we pray that you are able to find solutions to the problems that you are dealing with, and the problems that we, the emancipated women, are handing over to you.

God is the only true, authentic problem solver I can guarantee so, in every chapter, we study the word of God to get understanding and knowledge about how to live our lives. There is truly no other way to live life except to seek God's guidance. Powerful words are written in the bible. Proverbs 1: 2-7 echoes this sentiment precisely.

² To know wisdom and instruction,
To perceive the words of understanding,
³ To receive the instruction of wisdom,
Justice, judgement, and equity;
⁴ To give prudence to the simple,
To the young man knowledge and discretion-
⁵ A wise man will hear and increase learning,
And a man of understanding will attain wise counsel,
⁶ To understand a proverb and an enigma,
The words of the wise and their riddles.
⁷ The fear of the Lord is the beginning of knowledge,
But fools despise wisdom and instruction.

I pray that the message will be easy to understand, that in these pages you will find strength to make different decisions and choices for yourself and hopefully to stand taller than we can ever dream of and reach higher than we can ever reach. I pray that you are provoked by the Word of God applied to our lives in this book and realise that His Word is active and alive.

Also, smile!

Unless otherwise stated next to the text, I have used the New King James Version of the Holy Bible for referencing scriptures throughout.
NIV = New International Version
AMP = Amplified Bible

Defining the Problem

THE PROBLEM THAT MOST SOUTHERN African countries face – and you can easily extend this statement to include most parts, if not all, of Africa – is poverty. How the problem was created is different from country to country, but the intrinsic war we fight is poverty. We were poor for way too long, ruled by governments and leaders who saw Africa and its people as a continent to be exploited rather than receiving her onto the world stage in her own right, appreciated for her mystery and deeply buried riches. We have accepted poverty as representing what we are, what we have and what rules our lives.

Poverty opens too many evil doors, and when evil runs rampage in society we lose who we are. We were "ruled" and we were under another man's dictatorship for way too long. We were told who we are for way too long and, unfortunately, deep down where it matters, we believed what they said and are saying about us. The problem is that women in particular did not have a voice until recently. Even now it is a squeak that is easy to ignore and forget or argue away. Our hope, as women who are finding their own voice, is that your voice becomes louder and stronger and that, when you speak, my dear sister, the universe stops to listen and acts on what you said.

The problem is that we are getting older and as we get older we are beginning to compromise and accept some things as the status quo because we are tired of the fight and are just praying for a peaceful existence before we retire. We are not beaten by the system or politics or any of it. We are beaten by time. So, before we have fully understood who we are so that we can hand over a powerful baton to you, time has determined that our punches are not as strong as they used to be. Time in itself is not the enemy: the issue is that we spend most of it trying to find our place in the world and, even though it is not in full focus yet, we have to teach you how to be better than us as a womanhood. How can you win if we didn't do our part correctly?

Dear Sis, most of us were poor and had to spend life surviving instead of living. We are survivors. Our country is full of people who survived many terrible atrocities, both in the public arena and privately. My mother, my aunts, my sisters and I are all survivors of one issue after another. In my case, being the last female in my line in this generation, I had to survive the world and them (family) as well. Most of my peers are like me: we had to survive both family and the world and then try to put one and one together and succeed, have a name, a career, a way of paying our own *dang* bills, seeing as we thought *(we know)* that we are not "them". You know: "they" who had much more survival to do than us and therefore couldn't get as far ahead as us.

My dear sister, poverty is evil. It wraps you in all sorts of ills and misdirects people from the centre and truth of who they are. And our people had to fight, and still are fighting, obstacles that prevent them from tasting providence throughout their lifespan. Poverty makes one desperate: desperate to eat, drink, have clothes, learn, express oneself, breathe without fear of disease. It breeds all sorts of desperation.

The desperation drove us crazy. Desperation drives away love, integrity and honour and it blurs the margins between what is allowed and what is not. Desperation compels you to see the negativity around you and hides any positive elements. It will never remind you of who you are in essence, and what the good within you is. Desperation opens doors to all sorts of darkness and evil and mocks the light every human being has within themselves.

Poverty forced most families to live in different cities from each other, seeking employment. The well-documented migrant labour system is the name given to a methodical policy that started to chip away at our families. Because of poverty and desperation, families began to fall apart. They became torn apart by distance, coupled with lack of communication and the fact that the men were trapped in a system of insufficiency, where it would be easy for them to feel like they were not doing enough. The perpetual struggle of lack and longing easily made women disgruntled and bitter. Right there, our families were attacked and the family unit was never ever the same again.

Women had to work. This is a good thing under many circumstances, but not when undertaken in bitterness and anger. At work, women had to survive "working" and the "working environment". We became tough and, the more we survived and got a taste of power, the more our families fragmented. The survival mode and the struggle mode are not any way to have a Godly model for a family, to raise a family in love, peace, joy, respect and providence.

The system forced women to take a stand, assume power, become stronger and determined to see to the survival of their kin and the next generations. Women became powerful and aware of what they can do and what needs to be done. It was untrained power and oftentimes misplaced power. Fragmented families produce broken people. As women, we broke, but we survived that too and made a success of ourselves nonetheless. Generations upon generations, the evolution of women became rapid and drastic. We coined phrases that celebrate our newly realised power and strength. In Sesotho we say, *"Mosali o ts'oara thipa ka bohaleng"* ; in isiZulu we say, *"Wathinta abafazi, wathint'imbokodo"*.

We have realised who we are. We are our own women. We are no longer powerless and, first on the agenda, we are walking out of poverty.

With our new power and determination we can get bank loans to buy mostly things we can't afford and we have our names on doors of office buildings we will never own. One could say we have made it, but time is challenging us, so it is up to you to **live life** and not just **survive** it. My fear is that maybe we have not done an excellent job in showing you how to not fight and survive, but to live. Maybe we have left nothing for you to model and improve on, except the fragmented pieces of the things we have survived, yet my hope is that the very same strength we found within propels you higher into the wind. While doing it, smile.

Let me show you what I mean.

Economy

We have moved as a generation of women from the time when women were caregivers and home-makers to a place where women are CEOs and COOs and members of government in esteemed political offices, able to say, "anything a man can do we can also do". This is excellent. We are empowered.

Sitting in those seats are women who are up in arms, forming one social reform movement after the other, because of the pain they felt in climbing that ladder. We are sitting on our wounds and dressing them beautifully, and covering them with flawless make-up. Sacrifices were made, compromises were entered into, but the scars they left run too deep and it is hard to forget where we come from.

We want to leave you a legacy, so that you can do better and have more than we did. But we are also saying, "respect our struggle," and right there lies what will be your problem. We want you to "respect our struggle", know where we were. It will be impossible for you to do that without understanding our pain and seeing that we are right to still be angry at times when things are brought to memory. The Post Traumatic Stress Syndrome is real. It would be impossible for you to understand my struggle without taking some of my brokenness. So, we are setting you up to have preconceived emotions and conclusions about who you are in the world of economics. We are passing on what we learned to survive, but we are not yet teaching you how to live fully and prosper. We are not yet teaching you how to own the building instead of being employed to reach the highest level, "for a female".

When it comes to economics and money, you don't need anything that has to do with how the previously disadvantaged had to fight their way up. We need to teach you how to walk up on the side of the building, and then go straight to the top, with only a parachute for emergencies, and put your name on it. *Nje!* There are names for these things: they are "entrepreneurship" and "acquisition". It's time for a generation of trailblazers and record breakers.

Family

We were raised in close knit families. We pride ourselves for having the spirit of *ubuntu* (the spirit of unity, social cohesion, guidance, love for one another, a teaching spirit, a spirit that gives comfort when needed; the bible says all these functions are performed by the Holy Spirit.) We were raised to love each other, to take care of each other and all of us were raised by "a village", as the saying goes. But then we were too poor and the men had to leave homes and we had to work. Those who were left made sacrifices and compromises to feed their families while they changed who we are as a society. The Spirit of *ubuntu* left and we are now living in very small family units. Only those people who strictly have to be in your household live in your house rent free. We now largely live in a society where each man is left to his own devices. It is like a jungle and only the fittest survive. We have called this modernisation. Is it? We have survived, but I think the price was too high.

When the Spirit of *ubuntu* left, it seems He took with Him the essence of what family and unity is. We were a people that passed our principle from generation to generation, through our cultural norms and rituals. We moved as a people within the frame of respect. We had leaders and authorities that had held our truths for generations, and we lived life in peace and as a unit that was secure in the knowledge that you belonged to a people whose roots were deeper and broader than any single individual. We were all raised "within and by a village". Hard work was honoured and wisdom was esteemed. But then we became too poor and it became difficult. When it came to dying together or surviving alone, selfishness survived and families broke. It became permissible to scavenge another man's home in their absence, if it meant survival. The definition of what family is changed. It didn't all happen overnight, but the family that was was no longer: it changed.

Now, we have survived, we have adapted, we have moved on with the times. We also have cable TV (DsTV) and we see what other societies say family is: it is the "Modern Family" with the "Brady Bunch" and, if "Will and Grace" can call themselves a family, then anything goes. It has been decided that modernisation will speak louder than old truths. We have decided that the internet or bumper sticker statements that are made about family are true, truer than what we knew before. Are they?

We forged intimate relationships as persons when the climate of the day was telling us we were "lesser humans" because of the colour of our skin. We fought so hard to prove that we are as intelligent, as loving and as full of the Spirit of God as they are. We survived, but we forgot to live. Now our new families carry the signs of the fight. Now we carry titles like stepmother, stepdaughter, half-sister and, if not step or half, something else: the fractions, the fragments, baby mama, baby daddy, multiple daddies, all these are signs of how deeply we broke when our families tore apart.

Don't get me wrong: we are survivors, so we make it work. We smile on cue, and hold hands for social media and someone pays your fees and puts food on the table. And you are going to endure the dysfunction, as long as you are under our broken roofs. No wonder you are in such a hurry to leave.

Again, my fear is that we have not done a good job in showing you how to live in a family that is blessed, ordained and sanctified by God Almighty. We have not shown you how to live in love, respect and peace, to live so well that it is easy for you to reach out to another and lift them up and empower them. My hope is, even as we are healing our families, you revert back to the truth, and take for yourself the Godly family and nothing else.

This is my prayer for you. Please disrespect where we were in our broken state. Shame it and scorn it. Recognise it for what it is – a battle ground – and distance yourself from it. Ask that Spirit that our fathers had and carried to lead you to a place where they were before "they" drove us crazy, before we forgot how to love; that place where nations marvelled and spoke about the Spirit of Ubuntu that we have. **Don't survive love nor force a family: live it, be it.**

Defining the problem, I can go on and on and make the picture gloomier. But you get it. There are problems that are becoming epidemics in our society and it seems that we are running from the truth instead of solving them. We continue to bend the rules and accommodate the problems in the name of "liberation", "modernisation", "civilisation" or whatever fundamental theory you want to throw at what is happening today.

My dear sister, I need you to know the truth. It is an unchanging truth of God and the same Spirit that led our fathers to build communities in peace and prosperity for all, is the one that today can set us free from all confusion and plant us on a way of life that produces abundance and beauty in all we do. Most Southern African countries sang the hymn composed by Enoch Sontonga and parts of the lyrics of the hymn became part of the national anthem of five African countries, including South Africa:

Nkosi sikelel' iAfrika
Maluphakanyis' uphondo lwayo
Yizwa imithandazo yethu
Nkosi sikelela
Thina lusapho lwayo

Chorus
Yehla Moya, Yehla Moya
Yehla Moya Oyingcwele

It is my prayer and my hope that you embody this song again; not in tears, but in joy and peace, in a burst of laughter, as you, the next generation, loves and lives better than we did. I pray that you stand on mountains of economic and social reform and know that God is alive and has answered our prayers.

The bible says, in John 8:32:
And you shall know the truth, and the truth shall make you free.

This is a journey that I am asking you to take with me, in the wish that we break all myths and confront every lie that we hear and see being modelled until we live life and do not only survive each other.

Birthright

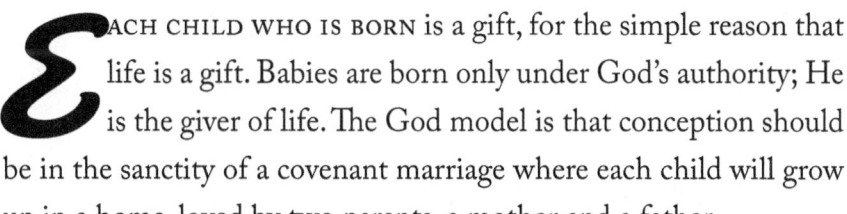

*E*ACH CHILD WHO IS BORN is a gift, for the simple reason that life is a gift. Babies are born only under God's authority; He is the giver of life. The God model is that conception should be in the sanctity of a covenant marriage where each child will grow up in a home, loved by two parents, a mother and a father.

The problem is that as humanity we have chosen to move away from this God model and have taken up options that are presented by modernisation together with science and these are framed as freedom to choose and the exercising of our free will. As a people, we have decided that we will exercise our right to choose to enter into sexual relations with whomever, whenever, however. It is almost as though we are saying, "Let the consequences be damned". What we almost neglect to emphasise is that free will is a gift from God and that there was never a time when we were not allowed to choose. It is what we choose that has changed, and not always for the best.

Another problem is that under unfortunate circumstances, when evil prevails, women and girls are stripped of their power and unsolicited sexual relations are forced onto women where conception occurs without their consent; they are abused. This happens in the context of forced marriages, rape, societal pressure and customs that still view women as sub-citizens.

Yet, no matter the circumstances preceding the birth of a child, each child born is a gift. No child ever has the privilege to be informed of their conception and as such every one of us assumes that we were made in love as God, in His will, allowed us to have life. If we were made in love, then each child born is a gift. It is only when love is replaced by hatred that a child will be born unwanted. Even then, God, Who is love, can change and move the hearts of people, and make them open themselves to receive the love that each child born carries and gives.

It might sound complicated. What I am saying is that, no matter the circumstances, you are a gift. You were formed in love and therefore you are a gift to the people who open themselves up to receive you into their families.

Governments recognise this statement to be true by establishing a set of "rights" under the child act that spell out the rights of children. These include the right to a family, nutrition, education and protection from abuse and maltreatment. This list is the bare minimum required by government law for the parents to provide for their children. If all is good and well in the world, a child who is born has a right to more than the bare minimum prescribed by the law.

Unfortunately, we have children born who cannot receive even the bare minimum.

Heavenly birthright - your inheritance

Sis, you should know what you are supposed to have received, are receiving and will probably continue to seek as a birthright when you are born under the authority of God Almighty, as a gift to your family and those whose lives were changed by your birth. Being born, just being born, gives you the right to require your birthrights from your parents, guardians and caretakers. If this is not given to you, they have failed you as a growing young lady; they have not done their part in activating within you the gifts of God that are as real within all of us as our very own DNA and genetic coding.

In society, a birthright is synonymous with an inheritance, or a sum of wealth to be acquired from parents at the coming of age or upon the death of a parent. A birthright that has to be activated within you comes from the hand of God in creation to you. It is not dependent on the circumstances surrounding your birth, or the wealth of the family you were born into, or on being the first or last child. Instead, it is a gift from the hand of God the Father into your life, confirming that you are a gift for being born. When you receive these gifts from the hand of God in the family you are being raised in, it is confirmation that He knew you in your mother's womb and gave you life. This is an inheritance for all humans from God our Father.

Being a gift

A gift is something to be appreciated and cherished by the recipient, and is often selected for its beauty, value and use to the person who will receive it. You are a gift. You carry beauty and value and you will add richly into the lives of your family and society. It is your family's responsibility to help you unlock all these as you mature, by availing to you what I call your birthrights. This is what is due to every child who is born; it is the instrument that each child needs to mature into a well nurtured adult who is a gift to the universe.

The bible speaks about natural birth and spiritual birth.

We are born naturally, on the day our mothers gave birth to us. In this regard the bible says our physical form is born into a sinful world and, as such, we follow worldly desires and propensity to sin.

Roman 3: 23 says,

For all have sinned and fall short of the glory of God.

And Roman 5: 19a, the scripture says,

For as by one man's disobedience many were made sinners.

Simply put, because one guy, Adam, in the biblical origin story, was disobedient and sinned, we are born into a world where people tend to disobey God and sin, and that desire to disobey God and sin is ingrained in all of us. We are born into a world where things are not as they should be. Our first instinct is to "fix" everything to our advantage and in so doing we sin, thus falling short of the glory of God.

However, as we grow and mature it is the responsibility of our immediate family to lead us into spiritual birth, to be born again into the Kingdom of God, where we are in tune with the voice of God within and can be able to access the gifts that He put in us when He formed us and gave us life. It is in this second birth, our spiritual birth, our being born again, that each and every one of us has an opportunity to access what God has provided for us, to live in a world that He designed, that we might be productive and be rulers. This is for all of us, no matter the circumstances of our physical birth. The birthright from the hand of the Father is made accessible to all when we are led and guided to be born again, hopefully even within our own families. But, if you were born in a broken family, when you pray for a surrogate family to lead you to Him, He will provide.

My prayer is that you grow up with the full knowledge and understanding of what you've already received from God as a child in His Kingdom. I pray that, as a young lady growing up, God sends light into your home; that, within an arm's reach, a teacher sent by God will activate in you all His gifts. I pray that you may embrace these gifts and live in them.

Romans 10: 8-10, 13 says

⁸But what does it say? "The word is near you, in your mouth and in your heart" (that is, the word of faith which we preach): ⁹that if you confess with your mouth the Lord Jesus and believe in your heart that God has raised Him from the dead, you will be saved. ¹⁰For with the heart one believes unto righteousness, and with the mouth confession is made unto salvation.

¹³For whoever calls on the name of the Lord shall be saved.

The bible teaches us, therefore, that God has put in place a very simple way for you to be born again, no matter the family you were born into. This simple way is, in fact, the only way. All it takes is believing that Jesus is the Son of God, and that God raised Him from the dead for our salvation. This you have to believe so hard that you speak, that you live, by it, and you pray that your life only centres around this fact: Jesus is the risen Lord and Saviour. By calling on Jesus, Jesus will move heaven and earth to be your teacher and guide, to lead you into full understanding, until you know that you are born again into the Holy Spirit of the Living God. That, because you are born again, what you need to rule and be productive are the gifts of the Spirit, the gifts that come from the hand of God, the Father.

This is how you can make sense of being born again and being filled with the Spirit of God. A building can look good from the outside even though it is not architecturally complete, and it might even function to hold equipment and be used as a store house. However a building that is designed to be lived in and accommodate more than just equipment needs proper plumbing and electric wiring. Without proper plumbing and electric wiring, the building will not be able to have heat and water and cannot be optimally used, even though it stands as a structure. When we are born physically, we have begun to exist, but we still need the Spirit of God to be alive and productive. We need the Spirit of God to live in the will of God and in purpose, and to be a gift to our societies as He has ordained it to be.

For this to happen automatically, it is the duty of your parents to love you, to teach and guide you, and to be there for you as you grow and mature until you can stand on your own. It is your birthright.

Then you do not grow up confused and lost, unable to find your place in the world. No child starts out lost; we get lost when we do not receive these birthrights.

1. You have a right to be loved

God designed it that children are born in the sanctity of marriage, in love, as a symbol of the covenant made in the presence of God between man and wife. Parents HAVE to love you unconditionally. It is your right to be loved. Love is that which envelopes you and forms an invisible cocoon of warmth around you, so you can blossom into the mature, beautiful person you are becoming. Love creates the atmosphere so you know that, despite everything and anything, all that is meant to be for you will be. Love is in the truth presented by the beauty in all things. It brings a sweet smile when you open your heart to it. You exist in love when, at the end of the day, you know everyone and everything is working as it should to build you up. You are loved when your needs are anticipated and met without you having to change the essence of who you are.

It is love when your life is full of light, peace and harmony, and leaves windows of ample possibility for tomorrow; when you have room to be all you can be and more without fear and shame. More importantly, you have understood when you know that God is love and is around you all the time.

Sis, you have a right to be loved unconditionally. By being born, you get to have someone who tells you, "I love you". That is how you experience God's love for you, by being told by a true heart. It should be the voice of your parent or caregiver, the voice of a true heart: a heart that loves you without expecting anything from you in return. When you experience what it is and how it is to be loved from an early age, and receive that love, then you are set up for life to be able to attract true love to yourself.

With the complications and intricacies of life, people can find it difficult to love others or to express love, even to their own kids. There are numerous reasons that parents and caregivers can use as excuses for not being able to love their children. All of the reasons emanate from the absence of love in their own lives. There are other emotions that can mimic love, but are not love truly. When an adult has not experienced love, or has not known love from a true heart, it becomes difficult for them to love you.

No matter what the reasons are, valid or not, understandable or not, it is the responsibility of each adult to work through their own load, fill themselves up with all that is Godly and be the true heart that you, as a child, will need in order to start developing the core of your character.

It is your birthright to receive love. Love is the double helix that forms the DNA of our character. It is this love that builds us to become who we are. Without love, any other gift or talent that one has will diminish in potential, or will be misused. It should be only in love that we walk towards being productive and ruling that which is allotted to us.

You were made by a loving God and that is your Godly legacy and that must never be taken away from you, by circumstance or actions. When you understand the depth to which you should be loved, and you receive it, you instinctively give yourself permission to grow and mature and become who God intends you to be. It is only this love that will repel any incoming form of hatred and deceit from derailing your life and changing your core. Receiving this love confirms the truthfulness of the inner voice within you, that propels you into becoming yourself fully.

This Love is within you. When it is ignited early on as a child, you do not have to go looking for it elsewhere. God will never run out of ways to show you how much He loves you. God will never be too far away to see your needs and longing. This love is abundant and only leads you to loving others as you love yourself (*Matthew 22:39*). Unconditional love quietens the doubt and sharpens our ear to the truth that **God is love, that He loves us unconditionally** as we undertake the journey of life.

As a born-again child of God, you have received a birthright to be loved as our Father says we should be loved. He says that He loved the world so much that when He saw the world destroying itself with selfishness and immorality, instead of death He gave to the world a gift of redemption. He gave us His only Son Jesus so that, instead of dying because of our lethal actions and choices, when we choose Jesus our natural course is forever changed and we can receive a new life and a new destiny. God loved us so much that He gave us His only son Jesus to die for us, but He rose again and took it upon Himself to show us the way to God by leaving us with His Holy Spirit to remind us that we are well loved.

2. You have a right to be raised up

Naturally, every living being changes with time. It was God who set time as a measure for creation and us in living in His universe to see the passing of generations. It is easy then to make a general statement that we are going to grow up. This is important for you to know as early as possible so that you don't become deceived into taking time for granted and assume things around you will stay the same forever. Realising that you are growing up also informs you to take each moment as it comes, to take full advantage of it by enjoying it completely while you allow the same moment to pass so that you can fully embrace the next. This sounds complicated: to be here fully and to see the next moment clearly and be ready for that moment. It is about being able to expand your mind and have the foresight to fully embrace the future, and yet to not be frightened about the fact that the number of our days pass quickly. The psalmist in Psalm 39: 5 says:

Indeed, You have made my days as handbreadths,
And my age is as nothing before You;
Certainly every man at his best state is but vapour.

It is this revelation that brings about wisdom. This is why, as a growing child of God, you don't have to know it all, all at once, and you have a right to be raised up by parents (or relatives) who cover you as you grow until such a time that the buck stops with you.

You have a right to be raised up.

The bible says, in Proverbs 22: 6

Train up a child in the way he should go,
And when he is old he will not depart from it.

If you are going to make something of your life, your parents should have the God knowledge that it is their responsibility to set you on that path. The other side of the coin, though, is that you should allow them to raise you, to teach you and to guide you. You have to be obedient and allow them to exercise their authority as parents in your life.

In our country, we find a lot of homeless children, a lot of lawless children, children raising children and irresponsible adults doing a bad job in some homes. This is not Godly and is a tragedy that is rooted in evil and not God. Even in situations like these, God is still in control. The bible says He is our Father who is in heaven. The bible also says He is God who is omnipresent by His Holy Spirit. So, even when the people who are supposed to raise you are not everything they should be, stay in the knowledge that God is everything you need Him to be in all situations, including your own.

There is a movie called *The Jungle Book* where a young boy, Mowgli, is raised in a jungle by wolves. The movie shows Mowgli mimicking the animals: he learns to walk like them, and he makes sounds like them and eats what they eat. In his mind, he is one of them. A tiger comes into their habitat and forces Mowgli to leave the wolves. When Mowgli matures a bit and in the face of challenges, he realises that he is in fact a human being but does not know how to be one. He can't walk on two feet or form words and use the full extent of his skills and intellect until, as the movie unfolds and one thing leads to another, he sees a human being and understands that he is capable of being more than he was raised to be.

Being raised up implies that, each day, there is a role model that you interact with with all your five senses; one that lets you know you are changing, showing you how you are changing, modelling that which you will become, setting you on a path to becoming better and bigger. Every child growing up gets to a point where they need to speak above their parents' voices and make their own choices and move in their own direction, at their own pace. That moment happens for all of us. Dear Sis, it is smart and wise when you postpone this moment for as long as you can. It is a blessing and you are very fortunate when you do not have to take this moment for yourself. This is one of those things that should be given to you.

This is the moment where your parents realise the fullness of your potential and they know that you have been set on a good path and that they have taught you every lesson they can teach. These lessons become *what you fall back on* for the rest of your life. When they have set your moral standards to a Godly level and have made you understand what it is to have roots, they have imprinted in you the knowledge of what is good and bad. The way that you approach life and interact with opportunities and challenges is influenced by your upbringing. It is a blessing when your parents have taught you above all else that you are a gift from God to them – and not only to them but to the rest of the world – and that God, Who is the ruler of the world, is the only One who can determine how big a gift you are.

Being raised up means being taught about the goodness of God. Learning that, even though we live in the world, we are children of God, Who is all good. When we know this and are taught this, then we grow up in His goodness. When we know the goodness of God, what our eyes see is immaterial. It does not define who we are, how we journey in life, nor dictate what we become, because we are covered in His goodness. In the goodness of God, situations do not become all-encompassing and all-consuming because His goodness surpasses any human standard. It is us taking His goodness and wearing it as an armour in life that shields us from the ugly, the bad, the dark and the cold of life. The goodness of God allows you to be in the world and harness its goodness to work for you.

You have a right to be raised up and to be enveloped in the goodness of God, so that you know that you are good, that you are a lady, that you are loving, that you have talents and skill to be developed and that, above all, you are a daughter in the Kingdom of God.

Are you being raised up or are you mimicking what you see, including things that are not found in the goodness of God? Growing up in a society where being *disadvantaged* is framed as if it is something to embrace, as if being *disadvantaged* offers more than normal, average advantages, is ungodly. In this environment, there is no shortage of really bad examples. We have people fighting or recovering from all sorts of past traumas and what you see is not by any measure what should be. What you see are people trying to do the best with what they have and they have never learned to be in a place where fighting or being defensive is not necessary. Dear Sis, you have a right to exist above and be more than what we could be. Being raised means getting you there despite what we have been through.

The only way we can raise you to reach those heights is to teach you about the goodness of God and to teach you to see His glory.

Sis, you are being raised up when you are taught about the goodness of God. In this way, the cup will always be half full for you instead of half empty. People who are optimistic tend to add to their own lives and to the lives of those around them. When you know the goodness of God and live in His goodness, you can change every situation to be as good as He is.

3. You have a right to receive

Globally, women can be recognised and applauded for where we have been and where we are going and how well we have done. We have worked hard, we are breaking down the walls of female injustices in most of its forms, albeit at a slow pace. We have shouted louder than everyone else about the rights we have and our shouting has made enough vibrations that we can say that we have a voice. This is good for womanhood all around. We have done well.

We have so many voices, even in our own South African townships and suburbs, that it becomes confusing at times to understand the message the voices are relaying. As a global village we look so superficially at matters and follow a course that shimmers on the surface and shout about "the rights" we have and "the voice" we now have and proclaim a win, but there was no depth to our course. At times, people are deceived into being in a temporarily euphoric state that comes with winning battles while the war is still ongoing.

However, the proverb warns that empty vessels make the loudest noise.

I point this out because, as a young black girl in Southern Africa, after hearing about your ancestry and predecessors who were counted at the bottom of the scale, you are ready to come up to the top, to be counted among the masses and be seen differently, often times at any cost.

Even though the podiums have been set and moves are being made, when we are all talking at the same time then no one is listening, no real changes are being made. No purposes are being fulfilled, the lost remain lost, the poor stay in poverty and those who dare raise their heads up are disheartened by the weight and complexity of it all.

Dear Sis, take a moment and listen. Develop your own vocabulary, look deeper than the surfaces, and then, eventually, when you do choose to take your stand, make it count.

"What does this have to do with receiving?" you ask. The answer is that you cannot give what you don't have. Our society is full of "courses of action" and you are here to propagate one or more of them. To be fully effective, you need to receive the tools you will need to make your mark.

Allow me to share this:

When I was around eight to ten years old, I stayed with *Rakhali* and *Mbiba*, my aunt and uncle respectively, while both my father and mother were somewhere else in South Africa, doing what were, to my young mind, very difficult to understand things. We were in a small, then new, suburb called Katlehong in Maseru, Lesotho, and we were surrounded by so much that I did not see then. We had a home, I had *Rakhali* and *Mbiba*, my aunt and uncle and my father's sister and brother respectively. I was sharing a home with my two cousins, *ausi Mama* and *Tebo*, we had food, and I was clothed and I was in school. I never went to bed hungry once. But I was so empty.

The reason I felt empty was that I was made aware by someone who felt burdened by my presence in their lives that my parents were absent. Their absence became the voice I heard and absence became what I saw going forward. *Absence* of love, of warmth, of friendships, of a hand to comfort me when I needed it and of someone who saw me and saw what I might need and of someone who was solely there for me. *Absence* became bigger than it needed to be, to the extent that, even in places I should have realised how full I was, I saw absence instead.

For you, my dear Sis, know that you have a right to receive.

For me it was difficult, as an eight- or ten-year-old, to make sense of things spoken and unspoken and marry them with things seen in reality. I was made to know that what I got was meagre and that, even though it was crumbs, they should have been given to those whose parents were around, raising them, being there for them. I didn't feel worthy of receiving anything given, and gratitude in me was replaced by confusion and a sense that I am deserving of poverty. So I withdrew into myself and I was labelled an "introvert" and many other unflattering Sesotho names that I have come to choose and understand only to mean "withdrawn" and negate the insulting connotations.

By the grace of God I connected to two things that began the process of filling me up, even though I couldn't at that age comprehend the spiral I was set to slip down. I connected with a love for reading books and the information and stories in them. I loved the feeling I got when I had read a difficult subject and had understood it. It made me feel different. It made me feel as if "I am better than where I presently stand". Secondly, I connected to God. In Standard 5, I joined the Scripture Union and I was taught and made to understand that God sees me and He guides me and is making me bigger. I understood and believed that He was making a way for me to have everything that is "absent" in my life. I was filling up and I didn't even know it.

It is by that grace that He made me "withdrawn" because, if I had roamed the world on my own, trying to fill up that *absence*, I would have found everything and anything to fill the emptiness that careless words had put in my spirit. God filled my empty parts; He made them well enough for me to be able to share of myself with you and with the world: share this memo with you. I have my own voice, I have my own vocabulary, I know what I am doing and I have enough wisdom to know He is still pouring into me and teaching and guiding me to do more.

This is my story. Yours might differ slightly from mine. It might not have been *absence* that rendered you empty and spiralling down a cascade. It might have been trauma instead, or neglect, fear, anger… any number of things that are put in us by the words and actions of other human beings and that leave us weak and broken.

There are many voices out there. Some of them make a lot of sense and the directions they point to might even look safe to follow. **The voice that you need to hear more than all others is that which God put within you.** If you are still standing empty, in confusion, with more questions than answers, and you hear a buzz around you, take a moment and ask God to start filling you up. God will fill you up by connecting you to everyone and everything you need to build your own vocabulary and have your own voice. It will not matter how far down the slipping slide you have gone, God can fill you up. **All you need to do is to receive God and His Holy Spirit will guide you into all truth.**

Dear Sis

These three things you have to know, understand, embrace and exist within:
- **God's love for you.**
- **God's goodness towards you.**
- **God's Spirit that is in you.**

I am praying that, when you have opened your mind to live in this knowledge, you will begin to live differently and choose differently and see all things differently; that you will start to see yourself as God sees you.

My dear sister, you are a gift, precious and wrapped perfectly by the hand of God, you are strategically positioned in your family, your suburb, your country. When you live in the love and the goodness of

God, allowing His Spirit to guide you, this is what your testimony becomes:

> *And we know that all things work together for the good to those who love God, to those who are called according to His purpose.*
>
> ROMANS 8: 28

Go ahead and say this simple but powerful prayer with me:

> Dear God, You know my heart and You know me. I come to You this moment and confess Jesus as my Lord and Saviour. I ask that You activate Your Spirit in me, that everything that is worldly and everything that does not come from You that spoke into my life until now be forever removed and silenced. Speak now, Lord, as my God and fill me with Your love and goodness. Let me never be the same again. In the name of Jesus I pray, Amen.

Knowing God, Knowing Yourself

WHO ARE YOU? MOST OF the time people give their names as the answer to this question. But we are more than the names we go by. Usually, in a social setting, when we talk about someone we follow the name with a physical description of that person and what they are commonly known for or what they do for a living. It is easy to conclude then that what we do, and even what we look like, makes us who we are.

Who are you?

It is assumed that, since you have always been in the same body and have in essence been with yourself all your life, you should know who you are, that knowing who you are should come easily. The question is, if this is true, how come so many people get lost in the sea of life?

We have people trapped in the wrong career, trapped with a partner who does not enrich their lives, imprisoned by the mistakes they made and living in regret because of opportunities they did not seize. We have people who go for decades, standing on the same spot and not improving their lives or the lives of those around them.

Without knowing who we are, it would be challenging to live our lives to their fullness.

When I am asked who I am, I say, "I am Rev Dr Pontso Phakoe. I work as an obstetrician and gynaecologist. I am a born-again child of God, fire baptised, washed in the blood of the Lamb." All true. But what I really should say is, *I am a light*. As easy as that. I am a light.

This is who I am, a light. When I say this, it causes people to start making assumptions and judgements. They attach some righteous standards on me and also attach their emotions to the statement: I am a light. It is easier for people to receive the first description, my title, my name, my career, my belief. YET, those things, good as they are, still don't define who I am.

Reverend only means I was admitted into an organised ministry and ordained a minister, in a church whose ministers carry the title Reverend. Doctor refers to the achieved level academically that carries the title doctor. My career as an obstetrician and gynaecologist is also a platform for me to be the best instrument God has ordained me to be. "Born again", "child of God", "blood washed", "fire baptised"… all that is what God did for me. All I did was to let go of my efforts and allow Jesus to rule my life.

I carry my family name, Phakoe. It is information about my lineage, the earth family that God placed me in. The circumstances of our birth and families we are born into are not a matter of choice. All families have challenges and I am sure there are a few things you can point out about yours that are not ideal. Our families influence how we think and behave, but certainly do not ultimately make us who we are. It is a blessing when you grow up in a family that is ready to offer you love, guidance and support and feed your dreams to take wing. It is a blessing when you have a family whose name has power to make opportunities to grow into yourself available. Ultimately, though, no matter where you start, we run the same race in the journey of life.

We have parents and guardians whose job is to nurture us to maturity and independence, so that we can begin to live our own lives in successful careers and happy homes. This is the golden goose. In the pursuit of the good life, there are certain trophies of life that will be emphasised, such as education, working hard, forming good relationships, reaching targets… and on and on it goes. This should be our way of life nonetheless, but not at the expense of losing yourself in the grinding mill.

Our parents, when we were younger, would observe our character traits, likes, dislikes and certain behaviours, and make generalisations and summations regarding our developing character and conclude that that is who we are. As a young lady you hear what your parents say in describing you and telling others about who you are and, because they are parents and they have authority over you, you believe them. Not all things said about you are correct or are influenced by Godly wisdom. Some of the things we have heard parents say about their kids include phrases like *she is lazy*. Therefore, as a child, you have permission to be lazy because you have grown up knowing how lazy you are. You will hear an uncle say about a niece, *she is beautiful and will have lots of boys following her.* This plants a seed in a young girl's mind that who they are is beautiful and men are a trading commodity.

We have also seen false positive affirmation on children cause disillusion and unrealistic dreams that lead to failure in life. Parents mean well. It is the job of a parent to nurture you to a point where you can know for yourself who you are. True nurturing that is done prayerfully and by the guidance of the Holy Spirit is powerful and prophetic to a maturing child. However, if what is said about you by parents and guardians does not align with the Spirit of God, it does not make it a reality. If you discover that there are certain lies that were spoken over your life, you have the power within to rise above them. Take a moment to understand yourself and truly seek the answer to the question, *Who am I?*

The truth about your identity

When it comes to the things that are manufactured by men, we would go to the inventor to fully understand what their invention is. For a really good product, people would want to have more understanding and they would go to the extent of wanting to know creative processes that went into the making of the product. We research the inventor as a person, the company and other creative minds associated with the making of this great invention. For example, we have movies made of Apple Inc's Steve Jobs, Google's Larry Page and Sergey Brin, Mark Zuckerberg of Facebook, and the Wright Brothers in the history of aviation. When we have a great product, as humans we go to the inventors for information about the product itself.

I have been an obstetrician for more than a decade and know, beyond the shadow of doubt, that a human being is a masterpiece made by God. No evolutionary theories, scientific ideologies or other religious myths should ever confuse the truth you know: **you are a masterpiece created by the hand of God.**

The story in Genesis, chapters one and two of the Holy Bible, details how God made the earth and everything in it, that He made man from the dust of the ground and then breathed into him so he became a living being. God still gives authorisation for every child to be formed in His own image and to be born by breathing life into them. You have been created by the Creator and if you want to know who you are, ask Him. The first step in knowing who you are is to seek God's presence in your life, to continue to ask Him who He created in you, so that your true identity can be revealed.

The bible says we are created in the likeness of God, in the image of God, as a mirror reflection of God. **Meaning who we are is like who God is.** Who God is is written in the sixty-six books of the bible, and if you have ever tried to read the whole Bible you know that it is a lifetime journey to undertake; that each time you read the bible you find something that seems as if it just that moment jumped onto the page, something you hadn't noticed before. So, who I am is who God is, who God is is hidden in a difficult-to-read book that is made up of sixty-six books and each book gives a different lesson from the last and defines God slightly differently from the previous book. Don't worry, finding who God is and finding yourself in God is one thing that is not complicated; it is not that difficult at all.

Have you ever seen a toddler? They have a perfect way of living life. What they understand is the need to eat, sleep and to be cleaned. They quickly devise a way of communicating to the caretakers to have these needs met, even though they have not mastered language yet.

As they grow, they begin to recognise their other needs and they also realise that there are certain things that they do that bring a smile to their caretaker. They begin to understand beyond their needs, but also that they can give something back in the way they behave. For a toddler, life is not about understanding everything all at once, but finding a serene moment in this place in time, where their needs are met and they contribute to the calm of the home. Taking a decision to understand who we are should be a journey with God and not a destination.

Most of us can recount a time where we came to appreciate the world and all the options and possibilities in it. It is easy to get lost in the confusion that is brought by ample possibilities. We come out as young adults from a family that had walls in place to structure our upbringing. These walls one day fall away as you grow older and discover that the world is bigger than the four walls that form your home. This is a critical moment to stand in the truth of who you are, otherwise the possibilities that the world has on offer will be overwhelming and lead you down a pathway of confusion. This is where you say, "I am ready to take a journey with God in discovering who I am". Each day spent with God will reveal more of who you are, until you can say, **"I am who God says I am"**.

This can be related to the bible story where God wanted to use Moses as His prophet, but Moses did not see himself as a prophet of God. At the time, he was a fugitive who'd left Egypt in shame and now found himself as a shepherd, far away from home, in Midian. God sent an angel to Moses in the desert at Mount Horeb to summon him and commission him as a prophet to be used by Him.

But Moses, who did not fully understand who he was or who God was, asked God:

> "Who am I that I should go to Pharaoh, and that I should bring the children of Israel out of Egypt?"
>
> EXODUS 3: 11.

He did not only ask God who he was, but also who God Himself was because he had not had a relationship with God before. God gives Moses the answer in Exodus 3:14, saying,

> "I AM WHO I AM." And He said, "Thus you shall say to the children of Israel, I AM has sent me to you."

Moses was both literally and figuratively lost in the Midian Desert, and God found him and introduced Himself to him. For some of us, the journey with God starts in a place where our loved ones would never have thought to look for us because, like Moses, we might have been and still are surrounded by controversies and scandals. We might be found with people we shouldn't be with, in rooms we shouldn't be in, having conversations we shouldn't be having, pursuing careers that kill us instead of being platforms to fulfil our purpose; but God came and introduced Himself to us and said, as He once did with Moses, "I AM WHO I AM".

It is a moment to hold onto, when your eyes began to see, and when your thoughts began to recognise that you might not know full well who you are and who God is. This is a moment when you received spiritual vision and your eyes can clearly see and your mind knows full well the difference between the lies that have defined you and the silent truth lying deep within. That is God introducing Himself to you, saying you are awakened to His presence, awakened to the breath of life in you: all you need to do is find that moment, that serene place within where all things become silent and align to the voice within you. Say yes to God and let Him speak and tell you who He created when He formed you.

Are you ready to take a journey with God and discover what He means by I AM WHO I AM, thus finding out who you are?

We understand that we are made from the dust of the ground and that God breathed into us to live. Find the breath that God deposited into you and only live as He guides you to. It is easy. The sixty-six books were not meant to be read all in one day, so allow the breath of God, the Holy Spirit, to teach you to walk in His ways. This is the promise that God has made towards you:

I love those who love me,
And those who seek me diligently will find me.

PROVERBS 8:17

You will find God when you seek Him. Start your journey by owning a Bible and reading it daily. Commit to joining a Christian group that teaches the Word of God. Commit to being a regular attendee of the group meetings and listen to His word and teachings. Make a pact with yourself to read the bible more than any other thing you read. Cut time from social media and use that time to be with God, reading His Word. After reading the Word say a simple prayer and ask for understanding. God will start to reveal to you the beauty of His glory and the beauty He placed in you. As you read the bible each day and you get to understand who God is, you will in turn get to understand more clearly who you are.

At times, we are so removed from God because everything around is ungodly and there is no glory of God in the immediate environment. It may seem as if the dimness consumes us and we fade away into our surroundings. This might cause one to start defining oneself according to the environment. We have heard it said that, if a parent abuses alcohol, the child will also abuse alcohol; a child of an abusive parent becomes abusive; a child of a mother who had kids as a teenager will also have a problem with teenage pregnancy. This is what a dim, ungodly environment would have us believe: that your circumstances make you who you are. But God is the maker of all things. He is the creator of heaven and earth. He was there in the beginning, He is always present now and He will be there in the end. God knows every possible statistic and probability, but only His Word will be sustained in the life of those who trust in Him while every worldly standard passes away.

Jeremiah 18: 2-6 recorded these words:

²Arise and go to the potter's house, and there I will cause you to hear My words," ³Then I Went down to the potter's house, and there he was, making something at the wheel. ⁴And the vessel that he made of clay was marred in the hand of the potter; so he made it again into another vessel, as it seemed good to the potter to make.

⁵Then the word of the Lord came to me, saying: ⁶"O house of Israel, can I not do with you as this potter?" says the Lord. "Look, as the clay is in the potter's hand, so are you in My hand, O house of Israel.

The prophet Jeremiah relates a story where God instructed him to go to the potter's house and observe the potter making a vessel out of clay. The vessel became ruined while on the potter's wheel. But the potter beat up the clay and made it workable again and created another vessel that seemed good. God gives this prophecy pertaining His children and we can apply it to ourselves as well. God made us out of the dust of the ground. If, while we are in the world, our environments defile and redefine us and we get lost, God is able to beat us into shape and make us into a vessel that is good.

Who you are is something that will change and evolve as you mature. You are a daughter and a sister; you will become a trusted friend and confidante; you will become a fiancée; you will become a wife and a mother; you will become a source of wisdom and guidance, a policy maker and a change agent. You will become so many things. All these changes have to happen. It is part of life and who you were meant to be. All you have to do is to guard that they happen in the hands of God. As long as they happen while you grow in Him and He reveals to you more of Himself, then we will never be confused by labels and external factors.

To Moses God said, I AM WHO I AM, but as time passed Moses was led into more revelation and he got to know God as:

The Redeemer

The Warrior, God Almighty

The Lord, the Banner

The Provider

The Saviour

The Healer and so much more of I AM WHO I AM

The Moses who stands on Mount Nebo (Deuteronomy 34:1), which is a different mountain from the one he stood on at the beginning of his journey in the presence of God, had walked with God, spoken face to face with God under the smoke of His glory, was seen by the nation of Israel as the representative of God. Walking in the presence of God had transformed him entirely.

So can you also be transformed. Your life will change when it is spent entirely in the presence of God: communicating with Him through prayer, listening and reading His Word, seeking His presence daily. I don't know about you, but my prayer for me and my house is that God transforms us as we walk with Him and that we get to understand who we are truly, not what happenstance had us become.

Who are you? The words of the psalmist capture the heart of someone who has walked in the presence of God and came to understand who they are in God.

> [13] *For You formed my inward parts;*
> *You covered me in my mother's womb.*
> [14] *I will praise You, for I am fearfully and wonderfully made;*
> *Marvellous are Your works,*
> *And that my soul knows very well.*
> [15] *My frame was not hidden from You,*
> *When I was made in secret,*
> *And skilfully wrought in the lowest parts of the earth*
> [16] *Your eyes saw my substance, being yet formed.*
> *And in your book they all were written,*
> *The days fashioned for me,*
> *When as yet there were none of them.*

*¹⁷How precious also are Your thoughts to me, O God!
How great is the sum of them!
¹⁸If I should count them, they would be more in number than the sand;
When I awake, I am still with You.*

Psalm 139: 13-18

This is the truth about your life. God knows you. From before you were born, He formed you. He made you marvellous and He put substance, treasures, in you for a purpose. My dear sister, you cannot look anywhere for answers that can only be found in God. You were made in secret; the secret is hidden in the heart God. Seek Him and He will reveal that secret to you.

My prayer for you is that you will know yourself beyond the worldly accolades and titles, beyond your primary needs, beyond vocation and beyond any walls put up by societal norms; that you will be found walking in God, will receive revelation that you are a child because He is our Father, that you are love because He is Love, that you a princess because you are a daughter of the King; that you are a light because where He leads you follow and bask in His goodness and mercy. May you know that what the lips of men say about you is nullified as you journey with God.

Dear Sis, you are a princess in my Father's house. Wear your crown with pride.

Let us pray together.

Dear God, I understand that who I am is in who You are. I pray, Father, that You will teach me Your Word and I will be able hear You speak. I pray that, as I learn daily, Father, You will give me understanding, that I might seek You with all my heart and walk in Your path. I humble myself in Your Holy presence and I ask that I live my life true to who You are. Amen

Hidden Treasure

*V*ALUE IS USED WHEN WE discuss sales. In commerce, value is quantified in monetary terms. So, the answer to the question, "How much are you worth?" would be reduced to financial notes.

We live in an era where translating individual worth has been perverted to a point where girls and young ladies pair themselves with men who can "afford" them in monetary terms, whether it is in extravagant gifts, giving them loads of money for favours or affording them opportunities that money can buy.

We live in a culture where we have put a monetary value or financial worth on our daughters. The culture of *lobola* is a ceremonial process where gifts are exchanged in the spirit of sealing covenant relationships between two people and within families; however some families have an almost unethical way of demanding money for their daughter's dowry, as if their daughters are up for sale. So we have, consciously or unconsciously, affixed a monetary worth to our daughters.

Don't buy into it, my dear sister. What is your worth? The simple answer is that you are priceless. Your worth can never be translated to any amount of money. Like the most precious gem stones, your value needs to be unearthed, admired and cherished, and then applied for the most exclusive and beneficial of causes.

Anyone who wants to offer you consumables or money to show you how valuable you are to them is certainly not worth your while. This ill practice of enticing girls with money is repulsive and should not be tolerated in any form or shape. Your value cannot be redeemed in a lifetime and those who want to share your life and all that you have to offer should be those who are ready to commit to a lifetime of living up to your worth.

These are three things that **could** *influence your self-evaluation.*

1. Family background

For at least the first eighteen years of our lives, we define our self-value according to who and what our parents are. We deduce our worth by adopting our family worth. A child who grew up in a squatter camp or any child who has a poor upbringing would be looked down upon by people, even by their own selves, as less valuable when compared to a child from a rich family. A child who grew up in a rich family would automatically assume a more elevated status than someone from a financially less fortunate family. Poverty automates one's mind to see lack and struggle and subsequently most people who are brought up in poor homes reduce their own dreams and expectations to the level of their lack. It becomes difficult to seize opportunities when you start to get comfortable in a depleted space and start to believe that your worth is reflected by the economy of your household instead of your self-value.

This is true when someone from a deprived family rises up beyond anyone's expectation. Then we marvel at their achievements and always underline that this is not the norm but the exception. So then it translates to the fact that, when we are from disadvantaged backgrounds, it is not that we are worthless or less capable than the next person, we just believe in our worth less. Listen to the truth that rises within yourself, that even though you are born into a family that did not acquire much monetary value and all money can buy, what your family accomplished does not entirely determine what you in turn will accomplish.

For a year or two, I lived at my uncle's home, *RanTefo*'s house, in an extended family setting where cousins from five of my grandmother's children were all growing up together at our uncle's home. My father opted to pursue a calling, instead of making lots of money. My father's choice became a burden for me to carry, growing up without necessities and what seemed readily available to some in my immediate circle. Growing up to live in lack sets others over you and takes away your power and ability to choose. You begin to believe that you are as small as they make you to be and as usable as they assume you are.

Maintaining your self-value means that you know that, even though you cannot presently change your family's economy, being in lack does not equate to giving up on your dreams, expecting less from yourself and allowing mindless people to abuse and use you. Self-value lies in the knowledge that you have enough within yourself to determine your own economy and choose which opportunities to utilise and which do not align with who you are.

It would be unfair to make a summation of my worth solely by what my father and family could attain economically, instead of what difference and impact my father made in the world and what was deposited within each of us as intangible value to tap into and ignite as we navigate the journey of life.

If this is your cross to bear, know this: your economy, your family's monetary value is a fluid, transient situation. Soon your worth will be incumbent on you.

Know that the starting position, where we have to reach within and access our worth and power, that position where we can all leap and reach out for possibilities, becomes equalised, one way the other. That position is presented to all of us, no matter where we come from and what our family backgrounds are. To each one of us is presented an opportunity that is sufficient to cause us to succeed and live in providence. This God-given opportunity is sure to come to all of us. However, for some people this opportune moment of our lives comes and goes without our taking advantage of them. Know this without doubt or fear: the starting position for you to leap forth into your destiny will come forth. The bible says, in Ecclesiastes 3: 1-2:

¹To everything there is a season,
A time for every purpose under heaven:
²A time to be born,
And a time to die;
A time to plant,
And a time to pluck what is planted;

There will be a time for you to plant, invest, put in the hard work and, in due season, that time will pay off.

The position where you can change the influence your background might have had on you presents itself in different forms, such as realising that you have a specific talent or gift and reaching into the power within as you start to walk your journey in life. When that happens, be on the lookout and ready to rise up to be the priceless gem that you are.

2. Friendships

Friendships can be a useful tool to assess yourself, and gauge where you have put your own worth at. You can do an exercise where you look at your friends critically and assess their worth. Whatever conclusions you draw, the same probably applies to you too.

Are they worthy? Are they helpful to anyone? Are they needed by people around them? Do they tend to cause chaos or peace? Do they influence their communities positively? Can you be sure that you will get good advice from them? Are they probably going to make a success of their lives or have they underestimated their own potential? Have they become stagnant and unmotivated to keep moving on and trying harder to reach newer heights? What is their worth? Because worth is a comparative thing, it can be useful to assess your own group of friends to see what you have decided your self-value is.

Your friends are people you talk to each day. They make comments on the sentences you form and put emphasis and importance on certain things you say and disregard other things you say. Surrounding yourself with friends who cannot esteem you will cause you to have a poor self-worth. The good thing is that you are not forced to keep any toxic friendships in your life. The minute you come to the realisation that the friendship is founded on you being put down, leave. The minute you realise that you have to compromise who you are and your principles to be accepted, leave. The minute you realise that the other people depend on you being weak and meek in order to relate with you, leave.

A friendship should strictly be with a person who will make the best decisions for both of you, will encourage you, will allow you to be yourself fully, and help you to work on your weaknesses. Young ladies deal with peer pressure way into their adulthood, keeping up appearances and façades for the sake of maintaining friendships.

Listen, this is too much work. Life is lived in the present, in truth, and not according to some elusive goalpost that changes every time you get closer.

Friendships are a place where you can draw great value; a good friend will add to your worth and not shatter your self-esteem. If you are still surrounded by such people, you are punishing yourself and probably allowing yourself to be undermined: leave them. Staying in a relationship, even with a friend, is always a choice. You have enough within yourself to be appreciated, admired and respected. There is no sense in undermining yourself to be a friend to someone who needs you to be less worthy on their behalf.

3. Interaction with the society

We all leave the comfort of our homes to become part of a society, whether it is in the schools and universities we go to, or work places we pour all our efforts into each day. In the era of social media, we don't even have to leave home to interact with society, the general population and with the people who don't necessarily form part of your small group or daily life. Social media allows the lines of privacy to dim and brings society into our homes.

In the yesteryear, even though you could not see all the faces in the crowd, there was a general murmuring in the way people are, or become when you are among them. They would accept you and you would feel their love, or they would resist you and you'd feel shunned, even though the words were not formed. Today, it is not a matter of feeling this and that; people reject you outright on social media and even go as far as to shame and attack others on social media platforms.

Living in a society tests one's self-worth on a daily basis. As a nation, as a society, we are moving from an era where the colour of one's skin would be assumed to equate with one's worth. All the injustices and ills of the past can sometimes be hidden in the intricate textures of our daily living, where gender, race, religious beliefs and so many other factors still tend to speak more loudly of our worth than what we have to offer. It should not be a factor that is on our conscious minds, as to how you fare in the world even before we prove our worth. If all things were fair in the world, the starting point should come easily, since we were called to live with one another in peace. But the stages of life are not set in that way. The truth is that society is pregnant with opinions and misconceptions; knowing your worth means that you understand that the society cannot change who you are and it cannot take away your power. You are worthy despite what they have assumed about you.

As a young black preacher's daughter, it took a while to understand that *He that is in me is greater than he that is in the world*, to borrow the words recorded in 1 John 4:4 in the bible. I have come to understand, and you also have to understand, the absolute truth, which is: **no matter which level society might slot you into, society itself does not ultimately determine what your worth is.** Instead, you silence the negativity and the pull-me-downs and stand in the power of Him, who is in you.

The only questions you should answer when you step onto the stages of the world are:

- Is your character honourable?
- Have you learned and developed your character to reflect the power and the light of God in you?
- Are you doing your part and contributing to the betterment of humanity?

Then, when it is all said and done, you are worth as much as you see yourself to be. You have to be fully alive in the world. You have to be fully ignited to realise all possibilities and be willing to step up each time when required to do so. You will make mistakes: forgive yourself quickly and move on. You will fail sometimes: pick yourself up and try again. You will meet hatred in different forms at times, but remember who you are and live your life despite this. There is an opportune moment that is coming your way. There will be a time and place where only you can rise to meet certain demands, right here in your own turf, a moment that needs who and what you are, just the way you are. The faceless crowd should never cause you to lose sleep. God knows your haters by name; let Him discipline His creation as you pursue your highest calling.

The truth about your worth

Money is printed on special paper made of a combination of cotton and linen. It comes out of the manufacturing machine as a blank piece of money paper. It then undergoes a series of intricate processes to make each note unique for the amount it is designed to tender. Different types of inks and drawings are used to differentiate currency respectively. When we use money, we do not look at paper notes of different values and expect them to buy the same amount of things. A R10 note does not carry the same monetary value as a R100 note because of the ink, the drawings and the markings on it, even though they are made from the same blank money paper. Paper notes of the same value, however long they have been in circulation for, do not change in value or depreciate, whether they are scrunched up and dirty, or clean and almost untouched. A R10 note remains a R10 note, even after being torn and patched up and folded over multiple times.

In Chapter Two, which deals with self-identity, we have established that we have the same Father, our Heavenly Father, who made all of us from the dust of the earth and modelled us in His image: the same blank paper. If we relate to the money analogy above, we then go through processes of painting and marking to have an outward portrait that reflects our value. By the time we are mature enough to be of service in the world and make our mark, the process that began with being born into a certain family, growing up in a certain environment, and being exposed to a range of external factors, has left an outward mark that can be read as our worth. Just as the value of money is not about the ink used on it, but about the product it buys, our worth is not about what we went through, but what we were designed to do.

I started high school at the age of eleven and my twelfth birthday would be during the school year. I had barely survived primary school, where I was terribly bullied and always harassed. I was young, skinny, with the coarsest hair ever, and I was way too shy. My two older siblings, *ausi Mama* and *Aihlale*, had already been in the same high school, five and three years ahead respectively, and they were "cool kids". I came in, expected to fall in with the cool crowd because the previous Phakoes were "cool kids".

Two of the most beautiful girls, *Katleho* and *Mateboho*, in the class of 1986 became my friends, and I was set to be a popular girl in high school. But, unlike them, I was withdrawn and too nerdy and a born-again Christian (having joined Scripture Union and loving it). Within six months of starting high school, social cliques had changed and I'd gravitated to the nerdy, praying bunch and my social standing plummeted. My two ex-girlfriends became well known and well liked and they ruled the school social scenes. They were always seen doing seemingly "fun" things. It's a good thing I moved down on the social scale, because I wouldn't have had money to belong to that group. I barely had any lunch or transport money to go to school daily.

I became depressed and more withdrawn than usual. I also started to be difficult to parent and I gave *Mbiba* and *Rakhali* lots of reasons to beat me to a pulp. Eventually, my father appeared from pastoral duties to come discipline me, and I was allowed to visit my mother regularly at the parsonage house in *Hlotse, Leribe*, ninety-six kilometres away, which was three hours by taxi then.

When I walked into that high school, no one could have looked at me, and decided I would be what I am today. I was too young, too skinny, too awkward, too shy, too poor and too religious. My look, however, was not my worth. Even now I continue to learn each day that there is more I am still going to do and I have decided where God leads, I will follow.

What is your story? What are you going through? What are your circumstances? All of that does not determine what you are capable of. All of that does not determine your worth. So again I ask, are you useful? Have you found a way to be a light in the dark, to point to hope in disillusionment, to fight even when the morale is low? **It is not the outward markings you have that give you value, but how you apply yourself and how you use the power within.**

There are a lot of very intelligent people who are known for their wit and social flare. But they do not seem to have any amount of success in monetary, material or even spiritual terms. We talk about how "smart" and "nice" they are. We all know someone like that, who seems to be able to hold a conversation about every subject on the planet and seem to understand the flow and rhythm of "things". You know, *mos*, we call them *abo-clever*. People like that often make some of the best entrepreneurs we know and become very successful. At times, such a person, who is often self-proclaimed to be smart and seems to be poised for success, will fall terribly and become stagnant in life.

It is important that, with all the goodness and worth that has been deposited in you, you understand how, when and what to apply yourself to. This is called purpose. We were not meant to "go with the flow" and waste away, chasing godless endeavours.

My dear sister, you were meant to leave a mark on your society and be productive. **When you live in your purpose, and pursue Godly goals and standards, your value multiplies**.

Whatever the odds that are against you, wherever you start in the journey of life, however many times you have to do the same thing other people did only once, we are all capable of greatness if we have courage. Close your eyes and think of a person who makes this statement true and whisper under your breath, "If so and so can make it, so can I". The outward markings that are assessed by the world do not really devalue your worth. All it means is that your **starting point might be a little behind, but that may also mean that you are in fact standing closer to the centre.** For you, God has made your destiny nearer compared to some. Your destiny can, however, only be manifest when you start moving towards your goals.

Zechariah 4: 9 – 10 says:

> *⁹ "The hands of Zerubbabel*
> *Have laid the foundation of this temple;*
> *His hands shall also finish it.*
> *Then you will know*
> *That the Lord of hosts has sent me to you.*
> *¹⁰ For who has despised the day of small things?*
> *For these seven rejoice to see*
> *The plumb line in the hand of Zerubbabel.*
> *They are the eyes of the Lord,*
> *Which scan to and fro throughout the whole earth"*

The above is a prophecy that was received by Prophet Zechariah to pass on to the children of God when they came out of Babylonian captivity and they were rebuilding the temple in Jerusalem. God was saying to them that, when they start to build the temple and their lives around it, they must not look down and be discouraged by the beginning, which always looks small. He says, in verse 9, that His hands shall also finish it. **God will finish everything that He starts and everything that He has put in your heart to do.** Do not be discouraged by the day when things seem small. Just start moving and don't stop.

With all that you have, pursue Godly endeavours and He can quicken your steps. Do not go on a journey to dig your self-worth even deeper into the abyss, but rise and know that even your biggest dreams can become reality.

Some of us go a few rounds, trying to use what we have to achieve our goals, and we get abused, we get lied to and pursue falsehoods, we get lost and disappointed and, after all the trying and the failing, one can feel worthless. But a dirty, well used, patched up R10 note is still worth ten Rand. In the right hand, any amount of money can buy an asset that can bring more worth. Are you in the right hand? God knows our worth. He knows your gifts and talents. He designed you as a gift to humanity. Are you in His hand? Can He use you? That you have gone around a couple of times does not mean that He reduces your worth. His mercy and Grace are sufficient enough to restore us and even add into us so that we are better than we were before.

You might be surrounded by people who seem like they have all it takes and are not dependent on God. Let me put it out clearly: all economies that are not built on good principles go bankrupt. The girl next door who seems like she has it all on social media and is not in the hand of God, will also dry up and run out. Do not be deceived or be tempted to run their course. **You are worthy in the hand of God Almighty. He will plant you in good waters so you are forever fruitful in your life.**

When God decides to put you to use, He does not look at the outward markings imposed by your journey so far. Instead, He remembers the truth about you that He created and starts to revive you up to the original worth He assigned to you. No matter how many failures you might have had, no matter the circumstances of your present situation, no matter the insurmountable challenges you face, when He calls your name up as His servant to impact the world, may your answer be, "Yes, Lord".

The bible calls it unmerited favour and the grace of God. All it means is that God will give to you a worthy assignment, a job, a task, an opportunity that, when He starts, He will complete. Trust in Him by being diligent and being trustworthy. The grace of God will point you to a big assignment that seemingly more worthy people should be doing; what it means then, child of God, is that you are and have always been of worth. You are more valuable than you think.

The story in the bible of a guy called Gideon is recorded in the book of Judges, chapters 6 and 7. It illustrates worth in the eyes of God. It tells of how the angel of God came to Gideon, calling him a warrior of God, even though Gideon had never seen a battlefield in his life. He was just an impoverished farmer who came from a lowly family. He saw himself as the very least among family members in a family that was counted as the weakest. Yet God put favour on him and elevated him and called him "a mighty warrior" and gave him a difficult job to do for the deliverance of His nation Israel.

The culture where people want to be esteemed for their outward appearances – their beauty, their money, their race, their societal status, their Twitter and Instagram following – while they are not at all beneficial to society, is an illusion and entrapment to keep chasing the rainbow.

In the Gospel of Matthew 10: 29-31 it is written:

[29]Are not two sparrows sold for a copper coin? And not one of them falls to the ground apart from your Father's will. [30]But the very hairs of your head are all numbered. [31]Do not fear therefore; you are of more value than many sparrows.

Jesus gives an illustration about two sparrows; that even though sparrows might be sold for the same price and fly the same, the one that is not kept in the hand of God the Father shall fall to the ground, whereas the one in God's hand is kept in safety. When we decide to stay in the hands of God, we are worthy to Him and He cares for each aspect of our lives, from the minor details, including the very hairs on our heads, to the major details. We are precious to Him, despite societal reflections. When God favours you, it is not for self-glorification but for the glory of His name.

The truth is, you are worthy and valuable. The fact that you exist and God placed you here is all the proof that you need. Society will have to expand its view and receive you at your worth and not the other way round. People around you must raise their expectations regarding you; they should be expecting more than what they thought at first glance. They should make higher and better pitches when they approach you.

The truth about your worth is that:
- Your worth does not depend on any external factors
- When you humble yourself under the guidance of God, you become more worthy than you could have become on your own
- Your worth is more when you are living in your purpose

My dear sister, I pray that you may know that you are highly favoured and esteemed. That you may rise and sit in the seats of heirs because you are a co-heir with Christ.

Let us pray.

Our Father in heaven, I am Your child and in me You have put Your blessings in abundance. I pray that You guide my steps that I might walk in Your purpose to be a blessing to others and my country as You will. In the name of Jesus we pray. Amen.

Eyes of the Father

SELF-IMAGE IS HOW YOU SEE yourself physically. No matter what the mirror and people might say about you, it is how you see yourself that is most important. How you see yourself determines the way you present yourself to the world. If affects your self-confidence and the message you put out to others as to how they are to treat you.

A person who sees themselves as beautiful, radiates confidence. These are people who are able to make good impressions on first sight. **Self-image, even though it is unspoken, communicates what you believe about yourself and informs the level at which you are able to interact with other people socially.** People who believe more in themselves and think highly of themselves are often afforded more of an opportunity off the bat than people who see themselves as faulty and less than perfect.

Globally, being "black" has been a challenge. We as black people have to teach others that the melanin in our skin does not equate to inferiority or any trait that makes us less human. We as humanity are understanding that we are all formed from the same fabric, and the details that code our individualism do not make one more or less human, just different.

We have moved from a time where our mothers' generation bought and used skin lighteners to peel off their skin to become "whiter" and scarred their faces in the process. We have moved from a time when no black super models were seen on major fashion magazine covers. The beauty industry has only recently moved away from anorexic looking super models and accepted super models who wear Size 8 clothing and bigger.

A little over three decades into a democracy, we are still babies in the ways of acceptance and tolerance. We have to learn in patience, to think differently about each other and resist the initial urge to judge each other at first glance, as history will have us do. This is our prayer.

We were judged and oppressed for so long on the basis of our looks. The judgement has left its mark on our souls. It is evident in that we have in turn learned to judge others back, on the basis of superficial, unimportant things, such as their accent and the way they speak, the texture of their hair, their tattoos, their weight, their cars, their clothes, anything external except what is important, which is who they are.

My dear sister, it is important to know that you are not the first black individual with curly hair and a broad pelvis who ever existed. You are going to walk into rooms where people will judge you on the basis of this for a long time. Women have then taken it to task to embrace their femininity. Black women in particular have stood strong so that we are seen for the goddesses and beautiful creatures that we are, in all our natural glory. We are presenting ourselves as we are and so the world has to accept us as sexy, beautiful beings, deserving of love and respect.

When you have taken up this ideal, to embrace your femininity and flaunt all that *Mama gave you*, let us agree there is a line, a position called self-respect that we have to honour. This is not about anyone else, nor about any system, patriarchy being the scapegoat we always bring to the slaughter. This is just about you respecting your own self. No one can tell you how to dress and how to present yourself. But whether we argue about it or not, **how you present yourself tells the world what you believe about yourself.** Think about it.

In a world where our vision is flooded with images on Instagram and all other social media platforms, on magazines and on TV, it is easy to manipulate people's perceptions with imagery that distorts reality and truth. There are apps that are designed to enhance pictures by application of light and colour so that the image is not exactly what the lens captured. The play of colour and lighting is used to make pictures that portray their own versions of creativity that are removed from the truth, to get you to accept the modified version as truth.

An example where the main truth in an image is manipulated with enhancement, colour and the working of light would be an advert that sells any harmful substances, like cigarette. We all know the harm and damage that is caused by smoking. The images on the adverts were never of a person in a hospital bed dying of lung cancer. Instead, the pictures were of masculine men and super sexy women in bright, beautiful, colourful clothing, blowing the most enticing smoke ever. The packaging of cigarette boxes was so nice (and I use the word *nice*, because using any other word would give too much credit where it is not due), until the weight of death caused by cigarette became too much to ignore. Now we have laws and policies for cigarette companies to say do not distort the pictures and images about smoking anymore. Make it clear what harmful effects smoking can have.

The play of colour and lighting can be used by the world at large to make images that sell and propagate their own falsehoods, to get you to accept what they sell as truth, even in the face of dire consequences. This happens in our own personal spaces, in our families and even in social interactions. We shade the truth with colour and distort the light so that the perception does not reflect the truth anymore. Be aware of these falsehoods and other deceptions that are meant to harm you, that distort your vision and aim to change your perception.

In the entertainment industry, when young female artists want to be famous their publicist work on their image to make them marketable. Unfortunately, the first thing they tend to do is to take off their clothes and leave them almost naked. What catches our attention is the nudity; the talent is secondary. This is now called *embracing their femininity* and distorted framing of what a woman empowered really is. Commercialism calls this *branding and packaging*. Before the publicist's interventions were applied, was the young artist not feminine enough? Before being packaged and turned into a commodity, was their humanity not good enough? The image they had, and the talent they want to share with the world, is it not good enough with clothes on? So the lack of clothing enhances the talent? The truth is that what the publicist has done is to change the lighting and the colours. With that our perceptions change and what we see of the artist is not a young lady or how they were raised; what we see is what the marketing intended us to see. Statistics will show that these human beings, these people, are not left unharmed by this commercialization and image distortion that is imposed on them as industry standard. With the money and the fame, they suffer from substance abuse, abusive relationships, depression and, at times, die in the prime of their lives.

We want to be in the world, looking our best and feeling like we embody the best version of who we are. Professionals in fine arts assess the quality of an image not only by how much of a copy it is of the original, but also by whether the essence, the truth of what the original is, applies to the image. **You want the truth about who you are to be what you reflect, even without uttering a word. This is important to someone who appreciates themselves and understands the value of self-respect.**

Here is the tough part that young ladies in these modern times find hard to accept: you have to respect your own self as well, as much as you want others to respect you. Identifying and understanding your true beauty means that you are able to present yourself to the world in the way you see your own beauty. You have to intrinsically honour yourself and hold yourself up to a place of dignity. There are clothes to wear that are decent and young and fashion-forward and cool, and that do not take away the essence of who you are.

When you go out for a job interview wearing clothing that do not make it easy to distinguish between you and someone who thinks way less of themselves and lives their life as such, you will never get that job. When you are in a social setting and people are looking to form lasting, deep relationships and you are dressed as someone who is looking for a superficial attachment, you will be treated like that. **Self-respect is that internal barometer that will make you feel uncomfortable in your own skin when you have tipped it over.** Listen to it.

We grew up with mothers who were made to believe about themselves that they were less than what they were. Our parents were people of very humble means. The systems of the past had put them in a place where they were maids and nannies and servant girls. They were made to wear attire that showed their meagre means and to behave as such in front of the self-proclaimed superiors. But even though they went to work in that climate, they understood self-respect and that the truth about themselves was that their spirit could not be broken by adversity and hardship. When they got home, they would lift their shoulders, raise their heads and they would dress up like *uMama, 'M'e, Mofumahadi*, a respectable queen of her own home, and not anyone's servant girl. This is the reason they insist, even today, that you dress yourself externally with dignity and honour and they insist that, even though you might not have as much materially, you make what you have continue to tell your truth: of self-respect, dignity and honour.

It is not about being born in this century, or decade. This is not about the level of education that we are able to achieve compared to them. This is not about us being able to do more in the work place than they could. If we assume that, we make the sad mistake of concluding that our human bodies have changed in form and shape since the last era! Have our bodies changed? Obviously not. What has changed is that, where they had to work hard to receive respect, we don't have to anymore, and therefore we take it for granted. Where they had to overlook insults and being belittled to gain dignity, we don't have to anymore, and therefore we take it for granted.

Honour is not a word used in our society anymore because *it is old fashioned.* Honour was celebrated by our ancestors and passed down the generations in all our societies. In the Zulu culture we had *umemolo* to celebrate honour, in Basotho we had the feast *ha lingoale li oroha*. My prayer is that, when the landscape changes and opportunities come rushing in, self-respect, dignity and honour don't leave us naked and exposed but that we clothe ourselves in truth, so that what we reflect is what we learned from resilient women, that their fight and strength was worth it; that we stand on the shoulders of giants and that their armour is not tatters in our hands but it suits us well.

If we truly understood this, we would get the hair out of our faces, roll up our sleeves, lengthen our skirts or wear long pants so that we can take longer strides, throw more accurate punches and go on with the business of owning clothing companies and building empires instead of having to stand on the same streets arguing about whether their fashion is old or not. It is hard not to respect a woman who is flattening mountains and raising valleys. It is hard not to respect a woman who is erecting monuments in her wake. *Dolled up* or *tomboyed*, let us refuse to be judged by the pretty pictures we make, but by the transformation that the essence of who we are brings.

> *The Lord God said, "It is not good for a man to be alone. I will make a helper suitable for him".*
>
> Genesis 2: 18 NIV

This verse appears in the creation story that gives an account of how women were created. Theologically, there are hermeneutical principles to be applied to this verse and to criticise it and compare it to Genesis 1:27-28 which says:

> ²⁷ *So God created mankind in his own image,*
> *in the image of God he created them;*
> *male and female he created them.*
> ²⁸ *God blessed them and said to them, "Be fruitful and increase in number; fill the earth and subdue it. Rule over the fish in the sea and the birds in the sky and over every living creature that moves on the ground.*

I want us to see in the above verses that we were created for functionality, to work, to be productive, to increase, to rule and subdue. We were created to be suitable in helping men, complementary and comparable, not less by any means. We were created into the same good universe that God created. The bible says our mandate is to be suitably helpful in productivity and God gave us the same blessing as human beings in this regard. Now tell me: when we were given such honour by God the Father, why would we take that away by assuming we were created to look pretty and be looked at only? My dear sister, I call you to take a stand. Don't be derailed and made to lose focus on finishing what our mothers started. It is not about what we look like; it is about what we do and, as a bonus, we can look good while doing it.

The truth about how you should see yourself

An image is what you see when you stand in front of the mirror. An image is a reflection, something you cannot touch or change. It is only real when you stand in the light, and darkness cannot produce an image. It is a reflection of that light that is registered by your eye that becomes an image.

It is important that you understand this sentence fully. **An image, although seen, is unreal** in the sense that, without the original object, it wouldn't be seen. It is not the original object, therefore its formation depends on the existence of the original form. It is not tangible and it can change instantly.

An image is formed when one stands in the light. Technically, all images need light to be formed. Whether it is the light that comes from a lens of a camera or natural light, an image cannot be formed without any light. It is how light is applied that changes what the image eventually becomes. The better the light source and quality of lighting, the better the reflection that is produced and hence the better the image. So what is seen, what is communicated to our vision, is the application and reflection of light.

If you want to know and see your own beauty, get the right light. Have God, as the source of light, to be the One who lights up your true self so that what you see is what He created. Have Jesus, who describes Himself as the Light (the Holy Bible, John 12: 46) light up your life and you will begin to see the beauty within and on you. When God is the Light in your life, it really does not matter the size of your nose, or the thickness of your eyebrows. When God lights up your life, you begin to love and respect yourself and that begins to transform everything and everyone around you to see His beauty and His image in you.

When your beauty is not lit up by the Light of God, but you appear on the world stage under a dim light, you are in essence only allowing a shadow of who you are speak on your behalf. The wrong light will distort your real image. People will not see the essence of who you are, they will not be able to read within you respect, honour and dignity; when your beauty hasn't been shone on by the Light of God, but is dependent on superficial things like dependence on plastic surgery, make-up and suspenders and people's comments and likes on social media.

> *³Your adornment must not be merely external—with interweaving and elaborate knotting of the hair, and wearing gold jewelry, or (being superficially preoccupied with) dressing in expensive clothes; ⁴but let it be (inner beauty of) the gentle hidden person of the heart, with the imperishable quality and unfading charm of a gentle and peaceful spirit, (one that is calm and self-controlled, not over anxious, but serene and spiritually mature) which is very precious in the sight of God.*
>
> 1 Peter 3: 3-4 (AMP)

The verses above teach us that we would rather have God enhance our beauty. We should not be so preoccupied with how our Instagram accounts are liked, or how dressing up to the standards of the world would enhance our profiles, but we should cover ourselves in incorruptible, unchanging beauty that is found in God. It encourages us to gentleness and peaceful spirits, dignity and honour.

Understand and know your beauty. Put it up to the Light of God. Therein you will find purity, decency and dignity, honour and respect, and an image that will not be changed by time and age.
Proverbs 31: 30 says,
Charm is deceitful and beauty is passing, but a woman who fears the Lord, she shall be praised.

My dear sister, you are beautiful, this is a fact. Those who do not see and respect your beauty do not deserve your company.

> Let us pray. Dear God, thank You for my body that your Word teaches me is the temple of the Holy Spirit. Father, teach me to honour my body, to treat myself with dignity and respect. Allow me to be what You spoke over my life in creation, to exist only in your blessings of increase, of multiplication, and of having power to rule and subdue everything you have given me. This I pray in your name. Amen

Self-correction

*M*OST OF US, BY THE time we hear the truth and understand who we are and our value, have already made a million mistakes. This is human nature. We made mistakes because we didn't know better, either because we were not taught well or because we let curiosity and peer pressure get the better of us.

Mistakes that girls make most of time cause pain that is directed at themselves. Mistakes that hurt the most happen when you gave more than you should have given. Life as a journey is full of a million wrong things that one can do. The ones we remember are those that cause a deeper, lingering pain, the kind of pain that even after years, when the scar itches, remind you of those experiences in the past that inflicted the most hurt. It is my hope as I write this chapter that you avoid those mistakes or that, if you've already suffered the pain inflicted by their consequences, you are able to heal from them.

Every child receives correction from their parents. We assume that with age comes wisdom and knowledge about life. Wisdom provides authority to say when a thing is wrong or right, and allows for parents and guardians to stand as a moral compass until each individual has developed within themselves the ability to make informed choices by themselves with confidence.

This chapter is titled *Self-correction* intentionally so that right off the bat the issue of judgement is off the table. We live in a society where people are very protective of their mistakes and if anyone dares correct them, we accuse each other of *being judgemental*. No one can grow and become better without correction. In the bible book of Proverbs, several verses encourage parents and children to love correction. Being able to receive correction and being able to correct oneself is of value and it is the foundation upon which a person builds their life. If that foundation is not based on a good sense of right and wrong, it would be easy to ruin and waste a life and embark on a lifetime of pursuing meaningless and harmful endeavours.

Proverbs 3: 11-13 (AMP) says:

[11] My son, do not reject or take lightly the discipline of the Lord (learn from your mistakes and the testing that comes from His correction through discipline); Nor despise His rebuke, [12] For those whom the Lord loves He corrects, Even as a father corrects the son in whom he delights. [13] Happy (blessed, considered fortunate, to be admired) is the man who finds (skilful and godly) wisdom, And the man who gains understanding and insight (learning from God's word and life's experiences),

As you grow older and wiser, I pray that you hear when you are corrected, without being defensive and trying to protect your mistakes. Mistakes that you defend will eventually destroy your life.

When we say self-correction, it is on the assumption that you have grown enough to have a mind that can be analytical enough to see a *line of truth* and see for yourself how close or far away you are from the truth.

The truth is not what the world says frequently or does commonly, but that which is wholesome, full of goodness and brings about peace, joy and love. Anything done that grieves your spirit, leaves you less joyful, causes pain to another, and brings a foul, dark mood is not the truth. Self-correction dictates that you are able to see clearly the line between truth and lies and be honest with yourself about where you stand. It means being able to recognise that some facts in life are a matter of good or bad, and black or white, while some facts are not but that the lines can be grey and that some grey lines fall on the good side while some grey lines fall on the bad side and therefore where and how you take a stand must be a conscious decision.

Putting it delicately

We live in a culture where a lot of things are permissible and there is not much that one cannot do or say. A lot of things that were taboo and frowned upon a generation ago are now acceptable. We also live in the post-traumatic stress syndrome era. Your parents, who were sensitized to pain and suffering, have devised means to shield themselves, and you by extension, from all pain – even *necessary* pain. Because of the harsh up-bringing of the past and restrictions that were imposed on us by poverty, illiteracy and colour, we as parents have found ways and means to make available what we didn't have and to have access to what we couldn't before. When we got to a place where we could, we professed liberty and freedom for all. It is that permissibility, in the name of liberty and freedom, that has enabled you to do more than we did, and this also means that you are going to make more mistakes and suffer the consequences of those.

By my definition, *a mistake* is something you choose to do and then you subsequently receive unintended consequences or an outcome you didn't think through properly. An action ceases to be a mistake when it is something that is thought out thoroughly, when the outcome can be easily foretold and consequences predicted, and only when that outcome manifests do you then decide to change your mind and wish you could turn back the hands of time. This is not a mistake; this is *regret*.

I know there is a thin line between a regret and a mistake. Both these are things we have all as human beings experienced and will probably continue to be humbled by. A *mistake* is often followed by *regret*, or in the worst case scenario by *arrogance*. It is not common for a *mistake* to stand in isolation without *regret* or *arrogance;* that is when people tend to protect and be defensive about their mistakes and are set to live a lie and to live below the margin of moral acceptability. It is important to know the difference between *a mistake* and *regret* because, although both of these teach us two different lessons on the journey of life, both of them lead to shame. The problem is that, if we do not deal with both of them on their merit, the shame can kill who we were meant to be and derail us for life.

Trigger: key to desperation

We all have a sensitive spot which, when pressed, causes an emotion to arise within us – be it anger, anxiety and fear, loneliness or any of the array of emotions – that will have us behave in a manner that we wouldn't have if all things were as they should be. This sensitive spot is called a trigger. It is the one thing that causes us to behave in a predictably erratic manner that, when we look back, we wouldn't be the most proud of ourselves and we know we have made a mistake.

When I was in primary school, I used to be bullied and for the longest time I, like most people who are, didn't know how to handle being bullied. I developed a good amount of suppressed anger and shame because I thought it was my fault that others bullied me. When I was in what is now called Grade 5, the kids who were harassing me and hitting on me almost daily gave me prior notice that I would receive the beating of my life that day. I was petrified and didn't want to ever go to school again.

Mme, my grandmother, gave me a hiding for trying to be truant and I had to confess to her that if I showed my face at school, "I was dead". She said to me, "If you don't go to school you are dead anyway; if they come at you, beat them before they beat you". So I went to school and spent that day in class in terror because I was supposed to receive the beating of my life at the end of the school day. That day, I allowed all the anger and embarrassment I had felt for all those years when other kids beat me and bullied me to rise up in me and I let go of it all and I hit another child so badly I had to be restrained. The bullies didn't see it coming, there were no adults around and they thought they would get away with beating me and putting me down one more time. It turns out that I was more afraid of my grandmother's beating than I was of them.

Expressed anger and fury felt good. Winning against people who had put me down for years felt good. Right there I had, unbeknownst to me, developed a trigger. For years, each time someone approached me in a manner that aimed to *bully* me, my reaction was fury. I would be sweet until you tried to push me down; then I would flip and explode in rage. As I grew older, this rage became a monster that even I disliked, yet for the longest time this was how I knew to respond to being bullied: with utter fury and anger. Anger burns everything in its wake and it took me a long time to work through it, to respond in love and patience in the face of pettiness and small mindedness, because that is what people who bully others are.

Each and every one of us has sensitivities that, when life has us walk past, we express an emotion that will alter our behaviour in a negative way, that what is we do subsequently is not what we would have done in the absence of the said dynamic. A trigger is powerful only as long as it is unrecognised.

When you look at and unpack all of your past stories from childhood, there will be a thing, sometimes several things, that if allowed to will have the power over the choices we make; the power to derail even the most conscientious among us. This *thing* is the trigger. Triggers include past trauma, like being sexually molested, or an absent parent, a broken or abusive home, extreme poverty and the list goes on. At times, a trigger can be something as soft as having workaholic and/or strict parents, peer pressure, chronic illness…

A trigger evokes an emotion within you that, when felt, produces a desperation that drives you to react, compensate and fill the inner vacuum, often at any cost, even if it moves one from that *line of truth*. When the urge brought by this trigger is indulged, you are on a path that is definitely going to be a huge mistake.

Common triggers

1. Hunger and poverty

Most women like me, who were born in Southern Africa in the 60s to the mid-70s, and our predecessors, had the same trigger: hunger. We were hungry for so much. Hungry for food and clothing. Hungry to change our environments and families, hungry for the promise of a better tomorrow. This was a common trigger for most of us on one level or another. We know that there is comfort in numbers. Therefore, because we were all experiencing the same hunger, dreaming similar dreams and wanting to get the same future, we were able to find rhythm in our quests and, generally, the desperation within us was well known and well-studied by generations of women so that, through shared experience and teaching each other, we were able to turn it into drive and purpose. Some, however, yielded to the hunger and, in satisfying it, made colossal mistakes that cost them their families and respectability. Way back then, mistakes that women made were not a slap on your wrist kind of mistakes. Then a mistake grew into an immense scandal in our young villages and towns and the load of such was enough to ruin people's lives – more or less what being exposed and ridiculed on social media does to you today.

2. Single parenthood and dysfunctional families

Most women who come out of the era of societal models that mimic migrant labour systems grew up without fathers. Lately we have found a way to popularise and *protect* this particular trigger. Absent fathers is not a new phenomenon, but in your generation, my dear sister, you have decided to use it to punish the mother who raised you despite everything, and insult an imaginary man, who might or might not be willing to take part in your life (a topic for another book). This trigger rests on the waves of hatred and anger and, as you allow yourself to become a male basher, or be an ungodly women who disrespects everything male by having immoral sexual practices, what was supposed to be just a trigger poisons your life and the decisions you make are born out of anger and hatred.

Every choice that you make that is informed by anger and bitterness is a mistake. When all is said and done, the mistakes it leads you into will only hurt and destroy you.

3. Patriarchy and racism

Being female, being black, having worked yourself to the bone to get here, can be seen at times by ignorant people as a disadvantage, as something that the powers-that-be have to remember when they discuss whether you deserve an opportunity or not. At times, my dear sister, we get overlooked and undermined and this can hurt the core of our soul, especially when we fully understand how hard we have already worked to be in the same room. Being overlooked, being undermined, being dismissed, can be a trigger that produces deep-rooted pain. There is a phrase that "hurt people hurt others". That pain can have you making a mess of your life, trying to find validation in the wrong places.

Changing the locks on desperation

If we are honest with ourselves, we would acknowledge that the mistakes we make follow a pattern. In retrospect, you realise that you might have made that one mistake one too many times, reliving the same dynamic over and over again. By asking yourself why, and seeking to tell yourself the truth, you are identifying the trigger that puts you in this place all the time. At times we have multiple triggers, but when you are honest with yourself you will be able to access how far away from the truth the triggers in your life have derailed you.

A trigger is only powerful, and continues to influence and affect your life, if it goes unidentified. This is important and sometimes this is so deeply implanted in our subconscious minds that it is not easy to identify. Luckily, professionals are available to assist. Most of us grow up without access to any form of professional help, but we have wisdom around us all the time – in our teachers, parents, guardians, *a village* that was willing to guide and mould us in love and care – so we become conscious of that line of truth that we all still have to toe.

You also have wisdom around you. Not social media or faceless advice on the internet, but people who are willing to pour into you that which can only be identified as wisdom from God; all you have to do is be willing in turn to open your heart to hear and receive correction. Once you are able to recognise for yourself what sort of things evoke a certain emotion in you, choose differently.

Self-correction is the process of having an honest conversation with yourself to identify what continues to push you onto a path that is labelled "mistake". When this happens, people assume that they cannot help themselves. Let me promise you that you can help yourself and you can choose differently. The bible says, in James 4:7:

[7] Therefore submit to God. Resist the devil and he will flee from you.

And again, in 1 Corinthians 10:13, that:

[13] No temptation has overtaken you except such as is common to man; but God is faithful, who will not allow you to be tempted beyond what you are able, but with the temptation will also make the way of escape, that you may be able to bear it.

So, you can help yourself, resist the emotion that the sensitivities evoke and be compelled to act only in love and peace. I know that for some, those who have travelled a long journey down the road of mistakes, it is not easy, particularly when we have already defended our behaviour and think that we are justified and there is a good reason to do the things we do. Yet, if what we do hurts us and those around us, we are wasting a lifetime away and living a lie. We all had to learn from our mistakes and choose differently. It is your turn to undertake each day, one decision and one moment at a time, to choose only from a place of love and peace and build your life on a foundation that is full of high moral grounding, integrity and a solid character.

Those things that challenge most of us, in this era where communication is easier than it was two decades ago, can be overcome more easily. We have platforms where these things are exposed and people confess that they are dealing with similar challenges to you. Why don't you find strength and assurance in knowing that, if someone out there can overcome this, so can you. If someone can rise above, find love and peace despite the triggers, so can you. If you want to disarm the triggers in your life, change the lock, change the way you react, stand still until that forceful impulse and emotion subsides and only act from a place of peace and love.

Personal triggers

We all have stories that only we know, stories that are real in our own minds but that can, however, be told differently by someone else. Narratives of things that happened and were seen by family members and neighbours and were experienced together, yet, the actual feeling and perception is known and only true to you. These stories are what influence and form personal triggers. Some incidents leave a dent on our souls that continues to nudge us to react and act in a certain manner that might lead us down the mistake lane. It is the feeling of doom and gloom and other negativity that these experiences brought, that remains alive in our memories and becomes a trigger. This includes experiences that one is exposed to while still growing and forming the foundations of who you are.

The same incidents in life are experienced differently, depending on our position and stature at the time. Each individual is positioned uniquely and therefore perception will never be the same. When these triggers invoke desperation, we can strip them down to fact and not feeling. Without the feelings, facts of a story can become unimposing and powerless.

I had a fear of being rejected and being left behind. I do not know how I got to fear rejection as I do not remember the first seven years of my life, save a few confusing memories. This is a documented psychological phenomenon – childhood amnesia – so I do not state it in pain nor sorrow; it is just a fact. Or it is probably related to my parents being away and having to stay with uncles and aunts as a child, but I know that in all my relationships I have hurt myself and others because of anxiety that I will be rejected and left. I only got to know this too late in my life, after I had made every stupid mistake in the book, by trying to hold onto wrong friendships and wrong people, trying to fit into cliques and to belong. The day I realised that I was made to be different by design set me on my path for my destiny and was the day I was healed. I stopped trying to fit in, trying to hold on, trying to over compromise. I simply stopped trying and I gave my life to Jesus in surrender and submission. I realised that it is my being different that connects me to my purpose. Now that I am at peace in this knowledge, people don't seem to leave anymore, and they want to hear what I have to say, and they seek what God has put in me.

For me, self-correction came after I had lost so much and while I was wallowing in my mistakes. But allowing myself to go through the process of correction brought me a new life: light, peace, joy and everything in between. Going through the process allowed me to finally be the mother my kids deserve, the doctor my patients deserve and the pastor my church needs. I have come full circle. I am a servant in the kingdom of my Father. Going through the process gives me freedom from my past, and my past cannot rise to try to pull me back, accuse me or shame me. I am thankful that God says, in Romans 8:1:

¹There is therefore now no condemnation to those who are in Christ Jesus, who do not walk according to the flesh, but according to The Spirit.

The process of self-correction allows you to leave everything that hinders and derails, and lands you at the feet of Jesus. He will give you His crown of glory instead of dust and instead of shame. The Lord will give you double honour and, instead of confusion, you shall rejoice and find fulfilment in what He gives you. The bible confirms this and in the book of Isaiah 61: 3 it says that Christ is sent:

³To console those who mourn in Zion,
To give them beauty for ashes,
The oil of joy for mourning,
The garment of praise for the spirit of heaviness;
That they may be called trees of righteousness,
The planting of the Lord, that He may be glorified."

Some life

Now that we have a pointed a finger at the things that push us and laid the blame elsewhere, we nonetheless have to acknowledge that our actions, when we have matured and grown up, begin with the choices we eventually make. A trigger is only powerful if unrecognised and unacknowledged. Eventually, even if people began understanding your struggle and initially understood why you make the choices you make, if you persist in giving your power away and persist in the behaviours you undertake, mistakes cease to be mistakes but choices and patterns of behaviour. You have matured and are ready to live as an adult and in truth when you know this to be a fact of life and the truth. You have matured when you can scrutinise your own self and correct yourself. The ability to correct your own self speaks to your character and shows the kind of person you are.

Some mistakes that we have already made are life-changing and have set our trajectory in directions we never anticipated. Jesus can work it out for you. He can. You have to be honest with Him and with yourself and walk from here hence forth in His Light. Dear Sis, some mistakes are life changing, no matter what your friends say. Some things are bad and harmful, and they will remain bad; they cannot be draped in any sort of modernized colours or repackaged in the name of freedom and liberty. Stay away from such things and be a person whose character people can trust.

The bible instructs us in this manner:

[13]*For you, my brothers, were called to freedom; only do not let your freedom become an opportunity for the sinful nature (wordliness, selfishness), but through love serve and seek the best for one another.*

GALATIANS 5: 13 (AMP)

Let me give an example. It has become popular for young ladies to call themselves "blessee", which is a new word used for an old, immoral practice where young girls provide ungodly favours to married men in exchange for money. Some of these women have tales to tell, and most of them have painful pasts that would shatter anyone's heart. I understand their pain and feel compassion for them. Their past is painful, their present is messy and usually their future becomes non-existent or not worth mentioning. A young "blessee", who never sees a line of truth and does not bring herself to self-correction, will always live in pain and sorrow.

Let me say it clearly and boldly: having sexual relations with **anyone in secret,** afraid of being found out, is a life-changing mistake. I need you here to exercise your faith and just believe me when I say it is a mistake. Read 1 Corinthians 6: 18-20 with understanding:

> *[18] Flee sexual immorality. Every sin that a man does is outside the body, but he who commits sexual immorality sins against his own body. [19] Or do you not know that your body is the temple of the Holy Spirit who is in you, whom you have from God, and you are not your own? [20] For you were bought at a price; therefore glorify God in your body and in your spirit, which are God's.*

Having sexual relations with someone in secret, afraid of being found out because you should not be with that person for any number of reasons, leads to shame and regret. This is something that you do to your own self and it is a mistake. The consequences of such behaviour will chip away at you and change who and what you are.

There are many other things that we do to ourselves and to others that change what and who we are, that change our characters for the worst. But Jesus can sort it out for you. Don't look into the world or anything that it has to offer; you will fall short and walk in shame and guilt. Only Jesus can restore you and take away your shame.

In the bible, Jesus narrates a parable of the lost son in the gospel according to St Luke 15: 11-24, where He says:

[11] A certain man had two sons. [12] And the younger of them said to his father, 'Father, give me the portion of goods that falls to me.' So he divided to them his livelihood. [13] And not many days after, the younger son gathered all together, journeyed to a far country, and there wasted his possessions with prodigal living. [14] But when he had spent all, there arose a severe famine in that land, and he began to be in want. [15] Then he went and joined himself to a citizen of that country, and he sent him into his fields to feed swine. [16] And he would have gladly filled his stomach with pods that the swine ate, and no one gave him anything.

[17] "But when he came to himself, he said, 'How many of my father's hired servants have bread enough and to spare, and I perish with hunger! [18] I will arise and go to my father, and say to him, "Father, I have sinned against heaven and before you, [19] and I am no longer worthy to be called your son. Make me like one of your hired servants"'

[20] "And he arose and came to his father. But when he was still a great way off, his father saw him and had compassion, and ran and fell on his neck and kissed him. [21] And the son said to him, 'Father, I have sinned against heaven and in your sight, and am no longer worthy to be called your son.' [22] "But the father said to his servant, 'Bring out the best robe and put it on him, and put a ring on his hand and sandals on his feet. [23] And bring the fatted calf here and kill it, and let us eat and be merry, [24] for this my son was dead and is alive again; he was lost and is found.' And they began to be merry.

The above parable narrates the story about the younger son who went to his father and asked for his inheritance from his father. When he received it, the younger son travelled to a faraway country and squandered his money on promiscuous living and being irresponsible. He fell so low in his choices and behaviour that the only thing he was good for, when all the wealth and people he had initially surrounded himself were gone, was feeding pigs. The bible says he was so desperate and in such poverty that he would have been okay eating with the pigs because no one gave him anything. In the desperation, he remembered who he was and made a decision to go home and beg for his father's forgiveness and even go as far as to say that, if his father was angry and disappointed with him, he could demote him to be treated as one of the servants, and not a son any longer.

This story illustrates that a mistake is something that can have many dimensions and deeper levels. Just when you think you cannot do worse, if you do not correct yourself and change your ways, there is always a deeper level that desperation can take you into. It shows that mistakes start with a choice. The young son chose to leave. Any choice that removes you from God the Father, is simply a mistake. Anything that removes you from the relationship and fellowship you have with God, is something you should not do. Out in the world, when you have undertaken to live away from the presence of God and do things that do not give Him glory, people use you and take advantage of you and the very same people will not think twice about leaving you stranded and not coming to your assistance.

The story, however, has a happy ending. When the young son remembered who he was, and who his father was, he corrected himself and went back home to his father's house to ask for forgiveness and his father forgave him. His father asked that he be given new clothes, shoes and a ring to show that he is still his son, because he was aware enough to correct himself. His father says, during the time that his son was away, living in sin and hurting himself, it was as if he were dead. He remarks upon his return that he was dead and lost and coming back home he is now alive and found.

In the preceding chapters of this book we have come to understand that we are children of God; that we have our heavenly Father who loves us and that He is merciful and He is our graceful Father. When we know who we are, even when we have made the worst possible mistakes, we can go back to Him, into His presence through Jesus His son, and ask for forgiveness. Like this younger son, our Father in heaven will forgive us our past mistakes and wash us clean and clothe us and dress us in His glory.

Jesus knows everything there is to know about all of us, even secrets that we have buried deep. He knows all that we fight and all that we face each day. He knows our thoughts and actions and yet, through it all, He would never condemn or blame us when we come to Him. He is the One who can forgive all that we have done and all we will do. Let's start today and begin to change and walk in His Light.

The process of self-correction starts with a need to change and the courage to make that choice. One cannot change unless the facts of the present reality are acknowledged in truth. You cannot change from a situation you pretend does not exist. Recognizing and acknowledging your present mistakes and their consequences leads you to repentance. You are repenting when you confess, lay out all your mistakes and make up your mind to never intentionally make those choices and repeat the same behaviours again.

Sometimes, patterns of our behaviour are difficult to change. This is why it is important that, as you change your behaviour, you also change everything and everyone that influences you to behave in that certain way. You have to change friends who encourage you into ill behaviour and decide not to frequent places that will draw you to things you want to see become different in your life. You have to sacrifice by giving up certain luxuries you might be used to.

In the process of self-correction, ask for help. Seek people who will understand where you come from and what you now aim to do and who will encourage you and teach you differently. Each day is an opportunity to do more good and choose differently. If you falter and fall back to the old habits, forgive yourself and try over and over again. This is how we grow to become people we were not before, one day at a time.

Let us pray.

Dear Lord Jesus, You know my innermost thoughts and secret places. You know the battles that I have fought and the challenges I still face. You know my strength and abilities. I have come to know that You are the only truth. I want to be like You, to live how You will have me live, to choose things that are found in love and peace. Dear Jesus, forgive my sins, fix my errors, build my character and ground my life in You. This moment, Father, I choose You as my compass and only guiding light, the only place I want to be found in. Amen

A Clean Slate

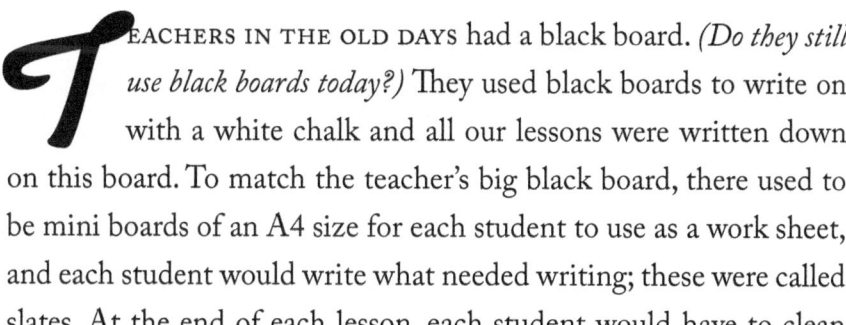

EACHERS IN THE OLD DAYS had a black board. *(Do they still use black boards today?)* They used black boards to write on with a white chalk and all our lessons were written down on this board. To match the teacher's big black board, there used to be mini boards of an A4 size for each student to use as a work sheet, and each student would write what needed writing; these were called slates. At the end of each lesson, each student would have to clean their slate to get ready for the next lesson.

We are born into a world that is full of sin and we are born with a tendency and inclination to sin. This we have discussed in the chapter *Birthright*. We are born with minds that are to be taught the things of God so that, when we mature, we grow in Him and live according to His word. Our naïve minds render us as innocent earlier on in life.

Our innocence is to be protected and preserved and parents have to teach you and cover you with prayers and equip you with the knowledge of God's Word to sustain your innocence. Your innocence should mature into righteousness and holiness as you learn more and mature in Spirit. The Word of God says we have to be holy and live holy lives.

¹⁴As obedient children, do not conform to the evil desires you had when you lived in ignorance. ¹⁵But just as he who called you is holy, so be holy in all you do, ¹⁶for it is written; "Be holy, because I am holy".

1 Peter 1: 14 – 16

This is something that we are so careful not to say too loudly because we have all faltered and sinned. God is a forgiving Father and we cannot live our lives feeling guilty about what God already forgave. So, those of us who have a long list of mistakes and sins that we have committed should be able to rejoice more, when we realise how deeply God loves us and how much He has forgiven and has removed from our rap sheet.

When we come to Jesus in repentance and ask for His forgiveness, He gives us a new beginning and a new chance to start afresh. Receiving forgiveness from God, by His grace, is an instant thing when we repent. There is no probationary period of assessment for God to see whether we are worthy of forgiveness or not. It is given to us by His Grace and on the merit of Jesus dying for the forgiveness of our sins.

So, no matter what lies in the memories of people who know your past and some judgemental people who might be looking for an opportunity to accuse you and to remind you of all that happened or that you did in the past, know that Jesus rebukes them on your behalf, because you are His when you have confessed Him as your Lord and Saviour.

The bible says that the work of salvation includes a spiritual cleansing, a redemptive process and a renewal. That means that when you confess to Jesus and accept His death as a price that was paid on your behalf, so that you can have a new beginning and a new life, He goes to work in your life by His Spirit to change you through and through – to change your behaviour, to change how you think – and, when you have gone through this journey by His grace, the old passes away and the new begins. You get to have a clean slate.

Most young people growing up in places that are dark and evil have their innocence stolen from them before they have a chance to see the light of day. These are places that are in dire poverty and people are desperate for some sort of power, even at the expense of others: places where gangsters and drug lords rule communities in the name of combating this poverty, and some innocents are forced into prostitution to put food on their tables; places where people are driven into all sorts of dark ways to make money and are ruled by a force that demands more, even at the cost of innocent life.

Innocence is stolen by acts of people who are so cruel and ghastly that they can only be described as evil. Innocence is stolen when someone violates you by abusive acts that kill your spirit and force you to be what you are not. People who are abused have to learn to cope and therefore have to adapt to make room for the pain and trauma from abuse. To cope, one has to change and often the resultant behaviour can further damage and injure the core of one's character and who you are. Abuse happens when the perpetrator acts towards you in a manner that produces harm and pain. It imprisons you in an environment full of fear and shatters your self-esteem. We have taken up arms but we have not been able to fight abuse as effectively as we should, but maybe it's the time, in a climate where celebrities are joining the war against abuse, that a radical change is at hand. Abuse doesn't only affect the individual for its consequences affect the whole society.

We were meant to have our innocence protected and live in a world where we can chose to do and be anything and everything that is in the will of God and is in line with His purposes for our lives. Abuse clutters your slate with pain, sorrow and darkness, and it takes away everything that lives in light, including laughter, joy, peace, love and contentment. It makes one's life confusing, directionless and disorderly and, when the trauma of abuse is given room and healing does not happen, one is lost forever in a life that was never meant for one.

Abuse has many faces and forms, but the common base is an evil desire and drive of one human to take away the power of another and render them weak and helpless to choose otherwise. Without choice, your life is open to being overwhelmed by anything and everything that perpetrators and people who will take advantage of your resultant weakness will throw out at you: insults, beatings, sexual harassment, being manipulated, being lied to and being taken advantage of in every single aspect.

We often are surprised when we get to know that women who look well put together and seem to be successful and seem to have everything going for themselves are also abused. This is because, even though abuse might be rooted in places of darkness, abuse wears a disguise and can spread into our societies like a potent cancer that desires to quench all light and hope in our lives, to clutter our outlook and remove all innocence that grows into righteousness and holiness.

In high societies, in the face of abuse, as an individual, sometimes we decide to cope and deal with abuse by hiding and denying and continuing to live as if it never has happened. Abuse is poisonous and, when ignored instead of being healed, it continues to render its victims weak and open to being manipulated, deceived and lied to and, at times, it teaches us to be abusive ourselves.

Living life under such a shadow of darkness breaks one's spirit, so that at the end of it all the burden that one carries is too great, and in retrospect it would be difficult to look back and recognise who you were and where the road that leads to the loss of all innocence began. It is not uncommon for victims of abuse to bury the incident so deep in their subconscious minds that they cannot even remember the abuse that happened, but instead find themselves indulging in destructive behaviour and attracting things and people who continue to abuse and undermine them in one way or the other.

Sexual abuse

A person who violates another sexually is small in their own eyes and seeks power by stealing someone else's innocence. There is no other way to put it than that sexual violence opens such evil in the life of the violated victim that it takes years before life makes any kind of sense again. Most victims of sexual abuse don't initially say anything, not because they can't or because there is no one to say it to, but because, when they can't immediately identify a place where what they've lost can be restored or someone who can restore what was stolen, it becomes difficult to make the words say what they feel.

Without healing and finding closure, the victim of sexual abuse replaces what was taken by indulging in promiscuous behaviour, in the subconscious hope that the void will be filled. This kind of abuse takes the vocabulary away, puts out the light where hope, love and joy dwell within, and plants fury and cruelty in their place. Darkness breeds things of the dark. Sexual abuse is evil and this pain does not heal unless brought to the Master, Jesus.

There are kinds of sexual violation that are not recognised as violation. Any act that is sexual or has a sexual connotation that leaves you less than what you were before is sexual violation. A man who manipulates and coerces sexual favours out of a woman by threatening her, or using his authority and power over her, is abusing her sexually. This masked sexual abuse, where you are manipulated and are afraid to say no, but you don't willingly consent to sexual acts, is as damaging as when someone takes from you by force and rapes you. Someone taking advantage of your weakness, brokenness and naivety is being abusive. Masked sexual abuse leaves its victims knowing that they were violated, but wondering whether they wanted to be violated.

A relationship that cannot exist on the foundation of the love of God but solely depends on you having to adapt and learn to make all sorts of compromises sexually is not holy. This is a masked form of sexual abuse, especially when you have expressed your feelings and have said no. The world will have you use the words like consent and age of consent, but any relationship that cannot stand in the Light of God is not worth being in. When that relationship is broken and done with, which it will be, only anger, bitterness and cruelty remain, especially when you consider what you were made to go through. This is the same result as if someone had taken from you by force and raped you. To fill the void, people tumble down a path of multiple relationships, as if one was violated to begin with.

The evil that is opened by sexual immorality breeds darkness and pain. Masked sexual abuse is equally as damaging as that which we have defined as sexual abuse.

When you begin a friendship that is meant to be courtship and in turn becomes a covenant relationship, which is a marriage blessed by God, but start from a place where you are filling the void produced by abuse, you are trying to have a thing of light but you are doing it in darkness. A covenant relationship, which is an institution founded in the kingdom of God, is a thing of light, but you are trying to have it in an ungodly place when you are just filling the void of abuse. Heal, come to Jesus, let Him fill you up with His Light, let Him clean your slate clean, and then everything in light will follow you.

When abuse has taken your power and your innocence has been stolen and replaced with exposure and knowledge of everything that is in darkness, the bible says that, when we come to Jesus, we receive the fullness of His healing power.

Luke 4: 18-19 (also found in Isaiah 61: 1)

[18]The Spirit of the Lord is upon me,
Because he has anointed Me
To preach the gospel to the poor;
He has sent Me to heal the brokenhearted,
To proclaim liberty to the captives
And recovery of sight to the blind,

> *To set at liberty those who are oppressed;*
> *¹⁹To proclaim the year of the Lord"*

In Jesus we receive healing for our broken hearts; we are released from the prison of pain and trauma of abuse, to see ourselves again in the Light of God, and we are enabled to receive our power back, so we can live our lives in love and light.

The world is careful not to say these things to you for fear of infringing on your earthly rights. If we don't say that there is healing, there is a place where your slate can be wiped clean and that you can restore your innocence and receive your power back, then abuse continues to produce it fruits of darkness in your daily life and eventually its burden will be too much to bear. You have rights. What about your God-given right to be raised up into the kingdom of God and your right to receive everything that God has in store for you?

Sexual abuse, in all its forms and levels, is evil. God, by His righteous judgement, will deal with perpetrators of these crimes. The commonplace nature of these crimes has made us numb and less sensitive to the horrendous consequences that this abuse produces. The consequent promiscuity that is born of this abuse is a present day crisis, the symptoms of which are fragmented relationships, teenage pregnancies, increased prevalence of sexually transmitted diseases, human trafficking, legalisation of forms of sexual immorality, and increasing numbers of sexual predators who are not prosecuted. All these are a symptom of our brokenness and anguish.

The law, together with society, has undertaken to put a Band-Aid on this deeply rooted problem. The Band-Aid is to separate issues and take one symptom at a time, and throw a temporary solution at it as if that means the disease has been healed. Let me look at a couple of these symptoms to illustrate the point.

Teenage pregnancy

Teenagers should not be having sex. This is my personal position. But because of the disease that is sexual permissiveness which stems primarily form sexual abuse, we are numb to sexual immorality and sexual permissiveness. Instead of simply saying to our daughters that they should not have sex when they are too young, unless they first want to get married at a young age, we as parents also abide by the law of the country. The law is complex and has several clauses and inserts, it is called the Criminal Law (Sexual offences and Related Matters) Act 32 of 2007, which has been amended. Of interest about the South African law in particular is the fact that teenagers are considered to be adults when they turn eighteen, but can by law have sex two years earlier without charges of statutory rape being filed. And then the same law has controversies relating to ages between twelve and sixteen, I really do not want to elaborate about these things; the point is that teenage pregnancy is an epidemic that is spiralling out of control and we as parents to these children have to take a stand that changes our children's lives, instead of reading about what government thinks when things have gone wrong.

In the face of teenage sexual activities, we have then as parents and teachers and society decided that it is better to prevent pregnancies than to have to change a behaviour that impacts all of us negatively, by teaching abstinence and preserving the innocence of our children (both boys and girls). So then we teach them preventative methods. When all that fails, there is an Act, a law that makes it a right for liberated women and girls at the age of twelve – and without parental consent – to have an abortion without mandatory counselling. If all that fails, we simply take the babies born out of this broken principle and raise them ourselves. We can't correct them out of fear of being seen as unsupportive parents.

Don't we think it is rather too late to be a supportive parent only when all else has failed? Shouldn't we be saying, "Be holy because God is Holy"? Shouldn't we be saying, "God forbid, but if the enemy comes into our home to steal, kill and destroy your innocence, Jesus can fill that void"? He forewarned us about it, so He can handle it. Shouldn't we vow that, through the help of His Holy Spirit, our daughters will be surrounded by mercy and grace until they are again whole enough to know that God can wipe any slate clean and give them a new beginning? Shouldn't our support be based on God, Who is our strength and pillar, rather than by putting on an ineffective Band-Aid on a deep-rooted problem?

My dear sister, I pray that you hear the words spoken here. It is now common to have teenagers having babies, but common doesn't make it right or good or easy. If you were given the grace to have your slate clean and free of burden, keep it that way. Stay pure, stay away from common practice and keep to Godly practice. I pray that you are covered with the patience that is found in the Holy Spirit and that you stay resilient in the face of pressure to conform and to be like those who are wounded and are doing what they can under the circumstances. When you have been given grace to stay in the Light of God, be that light and walk in it always.

Fragmented relationships

We live in a society where it is not uncommon for people to declare that they do not believe in the institution of marriage, yet they believe in love. These people forge alternate cohabitations that are not marriage, but sex can be had and children can be born without any commitment to love and honour each other in sickness and in health, facing life together.

People who confess that they do not believe in marriage often were hurt by their intimate partners or observed pain and anguish in their loved ones' lives, and now fear marriage. Adults who maintain broken homes are just outwardly portraying the brokenness and hurt they feel inside and exhibit the lack of trust that destroys any efforts made towards building a family founded in Jesus. Any children that are born from a relationship like this will bear the pain felt by their parents. Instead of waiting to heal even what might seem like the most superficial of wounds, we fill the void and settle at an incomplete place, in a fragmented relationship. We settle and forge ahead, when deep down we know the union is set to fail.

Eventually, one of the people, the man or the woman, will leave because there was no wholeness and two empty and broken people do not fill the volume. It is common for two good people, with good intentions, as it is in this scenario, to start out without recognising their brokenness and emptiness; to have their pain disallow them from having a stable, godly relationship.

Because of the sexual permissiveness we live in in this era, people are seen to have a string of failing relationships, each of which hurts and devalues them more than the previous one. In the face of broken relationships, the dysfunction and the pain become the authority in our lives. The drama is out in the open, for everyone to see in our societies, and we are very accustomed to it – baby mama drama, men are trash, maintenance courts – and meanwhile no one bothers to check on the well being of the kids who are now absorbing *(whether we like to admit it or not)* the poison that our anguish and cruelty is pouring out. Darkness breeds more darkness.

We use the law to cover it up – child protection laws and maintenance court rules. We resolve to forge ahead despite the pain and difficulties and stubbornly force relationships, even at our own expense – instead of solving the root cause of the problem, and declaring our emancipation and strength as women. We are forced by this fragmentation to raise kids who will also feel unloved and neglected by either parent and who will perpetuate the same cycle.

What if you had waited for healing to take its course, so that you did not attract someone as shattered as you are? What if you believed Jesus when He says He is a friend in times of need? What if your strength was shown by listening to advice when it was given in the beginning and your strength was seen in your humility when you acknowledged that you needed help? What if you were brave enough to show your wounds and you were wise enough to hear the truth that the blood of Jesus still heals?

What if we as parents were brave enough to encourage our daughters to wait until they see God in their prospective husbands? And we did not pressurise them into believing that not having a child (married or not) at the age of twenty-five means there is something wrong with them? What if we actually taught them that marriage is a ministry and singlehood is a ministry and that God has ordained each to the right people? What if we stayed with the truth?

When it comes to forming relationships, people look at how much baggage we carry. Even as a people we judge each other according to how much dust has settled on a person. Company owners have been known to show a bias, favouring men when they assign managerial positions using the excuse that theoretically men carry fewer life responsibilities, while women carry more because they also manage the home and care for children.

The baggage that we carry is from past pain, past mistakes, and acquired responsibilities that fall squarely on our shoulders. We carry a lot of weight as we live life and at times this can wear heavily on us. Jesus says In the gospel according to St Matthew 11: 28 – 30

> [28]*Come to me, all who labour and are heavy laden, and I will give you rest.* [29]*Take My yoke upon you and learn from me, for I am gentle and lowly in heart, and you will find rest for your souls.* [30]*For my yoke is easy and my burden is light.*

In the above scripture, we hear Jesus say we do not have to live this life journey by ourselves and that we can exchange this baggage and the burdens of life for His Word. He says that, when we give Him our baggage and take up His truth and obey Him, we will find peace for our souls, that our journey of life can begin to be in peace.

A clean slate means there is nothing written on this board; that it is unused. God can hand you a clean slate. Do not indulge in the things that people do that are contrary to the Word of God. Be holy because God is holy. We are children of God: healed, washed in His blood, redeemed from our sinful life, showered with mercy and grace and deeply loved by Him, the source of life.

> [25] *Since we (claim to) live by the (Holy) Spirit, we must also walk by the Spirit (with personal integrity, godly character, and moral courage – -our conduct empowered by the Holy Spirit) AMP*
> [25] *If we live in the Spirit, let us walk in the Spirit. NKJV*
>
> GALATIANS 5: 25

There is darkness all round. Let us get to work to teach our daughters and sons the truth.

Emotional and physical abuse

The bible says, in Proverbs 18: 21

> [21] *Death and life are in the power of the tongue,*
> *And those who love it will eat its fruit.*

The above passage illustrates that the words we speak have power and that words that are spoken have an effect to produce life and to produce death. This is true in life, in all that we do and in all that we say. When you grow up in the hearing of negativity and being constantly put down, you are being verbally and emotionally abused. They are killing your spirit. The tongue has power to build and to tear down.

The book of Proverbs 15: 1 – 4 says:

¹A soft answer turns away wrath,
But a harsh word stirs up anger.
²The tongue of the wise uses knowledge rightly,
But the mouth of fools pours forth foolishness.
³The eyes of the Lord are in every place,
Keeping watch on the evil and the good.
⁴A wholesome tongue is a tree of life,
But perverseness in it breaks the spirit.

Verbal abuse that stirs up your emotions is a sneaky pathology where a person is under the constant hand of an oppressor who uses a battering of cruel words to aggravate, to darken and to kill their spirit, using all means possible to make sure that they have no peace and joy in their life. This happens when you are living under constant insults and being undermined so that you feel unequipped to live your life on its own merit. The end goal is for the oppressor to have authority and power over you and for you to depend on them. The unfortunate reality is that, at times, the oppressors do not know any alternative ways of existing. This is when abuse has become the only state they can exist in and pouring out in anger and oppression into another person does not register with them as an abnormal thing or even as abuse. People who grow up under this dark cloud become emotional dwarfs themselves and grow up to become a shadow of who they were meant to be. People who were emotionally abused become reclusive and have to develop other unhealthy means of gaining their power back and expressing their emotions.

We do not appear on the stage of life wearing labels that say where we were and what was done to us, nor what we did in retaliation or to cope. A lot of people whom we meet and who are part of our societies have emotional scars of the trauma and abuse that they witnessed or went through themselves. The way they interact with others is directly informed by how they were treated and whether they were allowed to heal or not.

Vectors of emotional abuse

1. Poverty

For a child who has known dire poverty, it is easy to walk into an environment where one is abused emotionally without taking note of it until it has really destroyed one's soul. Poverty, if allowed to, ties too many ropes and ills of life together in a bundle that continues to steal and take away from its victims. The constant state of lack, emptiness and nothingness that is dire poverty chips away at one's well being and influences a person to see themselves to be less than what they are. If there is no voice to counter the sound of poverty, poverty can have you believe in all its negativity and have you seeing yourself as small when compared to others. Poverty itself can render one so powerless and voiceless that, when verbal and emotional abuse is directed at us, we have no power within to stop it.

The voice that counters the sound of poverty is the truth of God that we are worthy and full of His glory, set in His image as He created us. The truth of God is that there is no condemnation for those who are in Christ Jesus. No matter the lack, God does not condemn us when we are in Jesus. Therefore, we have power within us to speak against any form of abuse and condemning words that are directed at us.

2. Tradition and culture

Emotional abuse is difficult to speak of, especially in the black culture, because people do not understand that being a woman does not mean that you should be subject to being harassed and belittled by a man. Traditionally, there is a belief that wives are subservient to their husbands. This was true for our mothers' and grandmothers' generations and, by extension, this is what we learned. We were made to believe that a woman is like a child to her husband, and also that as a bride in a new family you are subject to literally all your in-laws and to everyone in that household. Only strong women were able to stand against this insane concept and then they were often judged as troublesome wives by society at large.

Another distorted culturally-based outlook is that in our cultures being single was (and in some places still is) seen as taboo, because women were believed to need a man to live wholesome lives. This is ingrained in our beliefs and, as women in general, it is easy to fall into an abusive relationship because of pressure from family and friends to make things work, even when one is abused. The fear of being single and being labelled as a failure, *lefetoa*, because one could not hold a relationship has forced women to stay in abusive relationships and suffer all forms of abuse for the sake of keeping up appearances. The problem is that, when this is modelled in front of our daughters, we teach them without words that abuse is normal and acceptable. They grow up to be abused because that's all they know.

Culture evolves with its people and tradition develops as we get to understand more each day what powers we possess. Men don't conform to the traditions of the past anymore, as households are becoming supported by women as breadwinners and women are taking more strides in occupying places of authority in the world globally. Women are not children and should not be treated as such. Any man who believes otherwise does not deserve to have a woman in his life.

Dear Sis, you are going to grow up to be a power house; a voice to be reckoned with. Let your *no* be *no* and *yes* be based on God and truth. Any word spoken to put you down and shame you is from the pit of hell and you should not honour people who speak death to you in your presence or with you as the audience. Walk away and shut up anyone, including friends, relatives and people of influence, who insults you, or harasses you constantly and aims to shatter your self-esteem. Anyone who can only ever criticise you and has never once given you a compliment is not worth your time. Don't take in their poison: shut them out of your hearing.

Physical abuse

Physical abuse is easier to identify. If they hit you, they are abusing you. It is easy to see, but still almost impossible to speak of. Women who live with abusive partners have often been emotionally abused as well and have no power to verbalise the abuse and they feel responsible for being abused, as though they have done something to deserve it.

Abused women become mean individuals and they raise mean children.

We are still standing in the streets and shouting as loudly as we can but, each day, women die at the hands of violent men. The root of the problem with physical abuse is anger and the failure to deal with personal issues that influences the perpetrator's own success and failures as a man and partner in a relationship.

Abuse in an intimate relationship

It has been said that women wear their emotions on their sleeves and that, when women love, they love hard. It is also how we express our emotions that makes us feminine and we connect with others on an emotional level. Often, when we speak of love, we are describing an emotional euphoria or infatuation which often subsides when real life events and challenges arise. We describe love as having butterflies in the tummy and weak knees and every reaction that is produced by a rush of adrenaline when we are excited. These are neurogenic emotions, not love specifically (see the chapter *Love*). It is on this emotional plane, this superficial feeling of infatuation and physical attraction, that oppressors take advantage to abuse you emotionally, physically and sexually, especially in a sphere of intimate partner violence. If we want to guard against abuse, we have to examine our own feelings carefully before we make life-changing decisions or enter into *permanent* unions with people who are narcissistic and are incapable of loving someone else.

There is a book by Robin Noorwood, titled *Women who love too much*, and there is other source material that accuses women of giving too much emotion and too much of themselves in a relationship. These are women who are likely to be emotionally abused, because they give from a place of desperation, in the hope that the partner will love them as hard and as much in return. These are women who get lied to, cheated on, manipulated and often financially taken advantage of. All this susceptibility to abuse is a symptom of broken self-esteem and a need for approval and to be valued and seen as worthy.

Dear Sis, you cannot be more worthy than how you see yourself to be. If you keep forging relationships based on how people make you feel physically, and based on emotions, you will be taken advantage of by those who see your brokenness and lack of self-esteem. A person who sees the depth of who you are, who sees your power, strength and your full potential, will find it difficult to try to tear you down with words and manipulation because they know that you will not stand for it.

1 John 4: 18 says:

There is no fear in love; but perfect love casts out fear, because fear involves torment. But he who fears has not been made perfect in love.

In an intimate relationship, the only thing that you have as a guarantee is words spoken between two people. Those words should be words to build you up, to encourage and strengthen you and to always bring you closer to God in joy and peace.

Everything that we think is eventually spoken and acted upon. Even pathological liars eventually reveal themselves for who and what they are. It would be wise if, when you meet someone to whom you are physically attracted and you are interested in having an intimate relationship with him, you surround him with people who know you and who can help you listen to his thoughts, so that you know his heart. If it is a heart of a man after God's heart, you will know and you can be sure that you are secure from any form of abuse.

Darkness cannot withstand light and any man who harbours ill behaviour and dark motives, God reveals. From such a man, walk away.

There is no woman who enters into a relationship for the sake of *whiling away time* who is not broken and does not harbour any anger, pain and hurt. Girls are made to attach to their partners. This is why girls talk of the wedding and kids and make ten year plans on the second date. We were made to attach to our partners and, for us, it's a lifetime thing. The only model of relationship described in the bible is that between people who are to be or are husband and wife. The bible does not describe dating and testing the waters while we give all that we have while we test the waters. That is the exact description of sexual immorality. This is what is commonly done and it is not frowned upon by the unbelievers, but serial multiple relationships are not biblical and are just a symptoms of how far we have fallen as a people.

In an intimate relationship that will become marriage, this is what the bible tells us to do;

> [22] Wives, submit to your own husbands, as to the Lord. [23] For the husband is the head of the wife, as also Christ is the head of the church; and he is the Saviour of the body. [24] Therefore, just as the church is subject to Christ, so let the wives be to their own husbands in everything.
>
> [25] Husbands, love your wives, just as Christ also loved the church and gave Himself for her, [26] that He might sanctify and cleanse her with the washing of water by the word, [27] that He might present her to Himself a glorious church, not having spot or wrinkle or any such thing, but that she should be holy and without blemish. [28] So husbands ought to love their own wives as their own bodies; he who loves his wife loves himself. [29] For no one ever hate his own flesh, but nourishes and cherishes it, just as the Lord does the church. [30] For we are members of His body, of His flesh and of His bones. [31] "For this reason a man shall leave his father and mother and be joined to his wife, and the two shall become one flesh." [32] This is a great mystery, but I speak concerning Christ and the church. [33] Nevertheless let each one of you in particular so love his own wife, and let the wife see that she respects her husband.
>
> EPHESIANS 5: 22 – 33

The model of an intimate relationship that you seek is that you will be loved by someone who will deserve your respect. You will be loved by someone to whom you have to submit, and that person will be your covering and will stand as the head of your family, just as Christ is the head of the church. The head of the family has to love you as deeply as he would love himself. He has to sanctify and cleanse you and make you glorious, spotless and without blemish. He has to nourish you and make you feel joy. This is the person you submit to. The bible says he has to love you as he loves his own flesh and his own bones. There is no place for abuse in this kind of love. He would rather sacrifice his own life than hurt you or deceive you.

My dear Sis, we have let hormones and infatuation, coupled with peer pressure and common custom, rob us of waiting in patience for the one that is after God's heart. Yes, we love hard. Yes we show emotions easily, but let that be towards a person who is worthy of our respect. You cannot submit to something that does not exist. A masculine frame does not make a man. A man is someone who loves the Lord and walks in His ways; someone who knows how to be your covering spiritually, to pray for you, to protect you, to build you up, to make you glorious and highly esteemed, forsaking all others.

Dear sis, I pray that:

The Lord God who is a sun and shield, the Lord give you grace and glory; that no good thing He withholds from you as you walk uprightly.

PSALM 84:11

I pray that His immense Light will drive away all darkness and give you healing in the name of Jesus. I know He will do it for you because

He did it for me. Often, all the abuse coils up and one can suffer all forms of abuse at the hands of one individual and also all these in a lifetime. I have seen much abuse personally, and I have experienced it. The stigma of abuse is in the why. Even today, I still ask, "Why?" But pursuing the answer to that question gives my perpetrators too much power and dwelling in the pain steals away from moments of my life today that are full of joy and peace.

Instead of telling you the gory details of the abuse I suffered, let me rather tell you how I am healed: He is called Jesus. I was steeped in a darkness that even I cannot understand and life was a blur of darkness. I had been exposed to too much darkness and my young brain could not process life. I became slow in school and could not write, even when I was already in Grade 3. I was very reclusive and was dying until Jesus said to me:

My word is a lamp to your feet and a light to your path.

Psalm 119: 105

This is how I lived, this is how I survived, by focusing on the Light that is Jesus. Taking each day at a time and growing to become who He ordained me to be, I forgot the past and I harbour no pain or injury from then, although once in a while a familiar shadow would rise in my life. When that happened, I used to hurt myself through ill behaviour. That gives those shadows too much power. In Jesus, in hope, by grace and one day at a time, you will not have to work too hard to forgive, because He will wipe your slate clean, He will give you new thoughts, new memories, new strength, a new character. He will make you new again.

Let us pray.

> Dear Lord Jesus, heal me. Take away my pain and mend my broken spirit. Make me new again as You remove all of what yesterday did. Give me a brand new tomorrow. Allow me to seek Your presence each day. Forgive me all that I did to myself and to others. Release me from the prison of abuse. Break me free, because he that is set free by You is free indeed. Wipe my slate clean and guide me again tomorrow as I begin to write a new story for my life in You. Amen

Love

EVERY YOUNG PERSON IS CURIOUS about growing up and finding that one person with whom they will spent the rest of their lives. Any other ideologies, where people choose not to have love in their life, come later in life, usually after a catastrophic experience that dissuades one from love as the ideal.

Love is the thread of connectivity that forms bonds between people, and binds people to God.

I have heard teachings where it is said that there are different types of love. I am not equipped enough to argue either way. For me, there is only one kind of love, called Love. This same love is experienced and expressed in many ways. Love is a threat that connects human beings to each other in the light and presence of God. The bible puts it this way:

And we have known and believed the love that God has for us. God is love, and he who abides in love abides in God, and God in him.

1 JOHN 4: 16

The highest, deepest form of love is that which you live in when you have a relationship with God. This love elevates you to know and feel that God is in the fabric of everything that exists; that God is love. Scholars call this *agape*, love for and to God. The bible says, on instructing us about living on earth, that we have to follow only two commandments. If we do this, we will find that we don't have to panic about hurting others and causing each other harm through hateful actions.

> *29Jesus answered him, "The first of all the commandments is: 'Hear, O Israel, the Lord our God, the Lord is one. 30And you shall love the Lord your God with all your heart, with all your soul, with all your mind, and with all your strength.' This is the first commandment. 31And the second, like it, is this: 'You shall love your neighbour as yourself.' There is no other commandment greater than these.*
>
> MARK 12: 29-31

The highest and deepest way that it is possible to love is when you love God truly. When you love and honour Him with every breath that you take, that is what it means to love God with all your heart, your soul, your mind and strength. Loving God is acknowledging His presence in your life all the time, fearfully respecting Him and obeying Him. Loving God does not equate to acknowledging Him for only two hours each Sunday, while for the rest of the time you are dismissive about Him and His presence in your life.

This is the beginning of all love, because this is the deepest and highest form of love. It is easy to understand that every other form of love is measured from and emanates from this, the love of God. There cannot be any other feeling or emotion called love except this. Any other emotion or feeling that removes you from the presence of God is not love and is not born of love.

How do you know if you love God?

The bible gives us answers to this question.

> ^{6}*This is love, that we walk according to His commandments. This is the commandment, that as you have heard from the beginning, you should walk in it.*
>
> 2 JOHN 1:6
>
> ^{15}*If you love me, keep my commandments.*
>
> JOHN 14:15
>
> ^{16}*By this we know love, because He laid down His life for us. And we also ought to lay down our lives for the brethren.*
>
> 1 JOHN 3: 16

Can you believe how incredibly easy that sounds? To feel the deepest and highest, most profound love there is, all you have to do is know the Word of God and follow what He says in His Word and walk in His ways. This is a very easy instruction and should be equally easy to follow.

Jesus is recorded, in Mark 12: 29-31, teaching us that to love God should be the first and foremost priority in our lives. If your life is difficult and dry and you need the love in your life, would it be difficult to take the bible and start reading to hear what more He says about following His guidance for our lives? Love is available to all of us. All we have to do is to open our hearts and receive the immeasurable love of God in our lives.

Walking in the presence of God allows us to know who we are (read the chapter on Self-identity). Allowing God to guide you enables you to live in your God-ordained purpose (read the chapter on Self-value) and having faith in God allows you to live in providence (read the chapter on Self-determination). When you know who you are, live a purpose-driven life and you'll know that God is faithful in all that He is and what He does. You don't have any reasons not to live at peace with your neighbour.

When you put God's love in the centre of your life it becomes easy to understand what Jesus teaches us as the second thing that we have to do after loving God, which is to love our neighbours as we love ourselves. The second instruction has two parts to it:

i. Love yourself
ii. Love your neighbour as you love yourself.

When we have the love of God, which is immeasurable, it becomes easy to share that same love with other people.

> *^{31}And the second, like it, is this: 'You shall love your neighbour as yourself.'*
> *There is no other commandment greater than these.*
>
> MARK 12: 31

Love is a thread that connects human beings together. Jesus teaches us to love each other by treating another person the way you would want to be treated. This is the second level of love: loving others with a pure heart, a heart that is found in God.

Loving others with a pure heart is described in 1 Corinthians 13: 4-7, which says:

> *^{4}Love suffers long and is kind; love does not envy; love does not parade itself, is not puffed up; ^{5}does not behave rudely, does not seek its own, is*

not provoked, thinks no evil, ⁶does not rejoice in iniquity, but rejoices in the truth; ⁷bears all things, believes all things, hopes all things, endures all things.

I want to propose to you that this is all the love there is. In the love that is rooted in God the Father is found kindness, humility, selflessness, patience, strength and truth. The other forms of feeling and expressions of emotion that are unlike what is described above are something other than the Love of God.

¹⁵Do not love the world or the things in the world. If anyone loves the world, the love of the Father is not in him. ¹⁶For all that is in the world- the lust of the flesh, the lust of the eyes, and the pride of life-is not of the Father but is of the world. ¹⁷And the world is passing away, and the lust of it; but he who does the will of God abides forever.

1 JOHN 2: 15 – 17

Any form of emotion whose expression starts outside of the love of God is not love. These are forms of feeling and emotion that mimic love, although they are not love.

Reality check

I remember being a teenager and packing my very few belongings and heading off to university. *Mbiba* was a man of very few, but powerful, words. When I left home at the age of seventeen to go to university, *Mbiba* said to me that "I must use my head and make sure

I pass". That is all the *being talked to* I got as a send off as I left home at the ripe old age of seventeen.

I succeeded academically, but I made every other mistake in the book. In our day we did not have Life Orientation as a subject, there was no social media, and in fact no TV available to many of us. For me specifically, I didn't see parents at home modelling for me what I might understand as love in the common meaning of the word (my parents being away, being good pastors and all). The only close relatives who were a couple and who were in my proximity demonstrated the classic, text book definition of abuse. I am saying that, for the longest time, I got it very twisted in my understanding of what love is.

The only information I had from life was from the *Mills & Boon* fiction novels. If you have read those novels, you will remember that this is how it goes in the *Mills & Boon* world: girl is in trouble; girl meets boy; they go through challenges; boy becomes knight in shining armour, and then, voilà, they live happily ever after. You see! So it seemed to me that, since it felt like I was in trouble all the time, what with dire poverty and absent parents, I was a candidate to be found by my prince charming, as was clearly described over and over again in *Mills & Boon*.

No one had ever taught me what love was truly. No one had ever said that God is Love, and that if I live in Him, then I am in Love. I received Jesus as my Lord and Saviour at the age of nine and was being taught His Word and was walking in His Light. I was in Love. But I still did not fully understand that I didn't have to turn twenty-one years old and then give myself permission to sin, in the name of "finding love", when I'd never lost it to start with. No one had ever said that I don't need anyone – neither a frog nor Prince Charming – to find me, since I was in fact not lost.

You have your own reality to contend with. You might not have been taught, and you might not have received Jesus as Lord and Saviour; it might be that you had no role models to show you what love looks like. There are many reasons we do what we do, why we allow ourselves to go through what we do.

The reality that I see daily is that more babies are born before marriage than ever before. This is not taboo any more. The reality is that government allows the age of sexual consent in South Africa to be sixteen years. The reality is that abortion is legal to children of the age of twelve. The reality is that we have adopted a new language for the lifestyle that has been adopted – baby mama, baby daddy (so to differentiate between the real Mum and not Dad) – and the maintenance court is overcrowded simply because we did not understand this:

> [29]...."*The first of all the commandments is: 'Hear, O Israel, the Lord our God, the Lord is one.* [30]*And you shall love the Lord your God with all your heart, with all your soul, with all your mind, and with all your strength.' This is the first commandment.* [31]*And the second, like it, is this: 'You shall love your neighbour as yourself.' There is no other commandment greater than these.*
>
> MARK 12: 29-31

The question for every young lady should be, "How do we conduct ourselves before we are married?" That should be the question, but instead questions that are commonly raised are, how do you get him (the guy that has left) to support the child? How do you deal with baby mama? If he has another woman, are you to fight for him? If he has disappeared, how long should you wait for him?

These questions break my heart, because these are not questions that are supposed to be asked by someone who knows what love is or someone who has the love of God in their lives. These are questions that are asked by someone who is so broken that they do not know what love is or how to love and be loved. These are born from fear and confusion, which the scripture teaches are not love. 1 John 4: 18-21

> *[18]There is no fear in love; but perfect love casts out fear, because fear involves torment. But he who fears has not been made perfect in love. [19]We love Him because he first loved us. [20]if someone says, "I love God," and hates his brother, he is a liar; for he who does not love his brother whom he has seen, how can he love God whom he has not seen? [21]And this commandment we have from Him: that he who loves God must love his brother also."*

I am therefore giving an in depth teaching directly from the Word of God so that we gain full knowledge and understanding of what love is. We have too many sources that teach us and model for us the wrong things about love. We are flooded by pictures of lust, greed, adultery, theft, desperation, abuse, brokenness, and so much more all masked to imitate love, all of which lead to heartbreak and more brokenness. So, in this chapter, we will intentionally go deeper into the Word of God to correct any misconceptions and bring us to the truth that we should apply into our lives.

When I began, I said that the love of God is the only type of love I can vouch for and I explained that the depth to which this love is experienced is what might be described by some as "different kinds of love".

The introduction of this chapter deals with the love of God, as both the deepest and highest form of love. The love of God should be the centre of our livelihood. The second way to experience love is the love for oneself, intrinsic love, and the third way to experience love is when we love others, shared love. Whether intrinsic or in loving others, all love comes from God, because God is love.

Intrinsic love

We experience love intrinsically, when we know how to love ourselves. That intrinsic love can only be received from God. It is this love that we display in how we love others when we start to form our own relationships. We have delved into this intrinsic love in the first chapter of this book, *Birthright*. God uses parents and guardians in a child's life early on to build up the fibre of this love. God loves us immensely and He wants this truth to be the foundation that causes us to mature to be who we are becoming. He sets us in families whose mandate is to express this kind of love that is poured into us by God the Father.

The love of God is a giving kind of love. John 3: 16, quoted below, says:

For God so loved the world that He gave His only begotten Son, that whoever believes in Him should not perish but have everlasting life.

When we have received the love of God as children, we know that in love we receive without cost. We receive kindness, humility, selflessness, patience, strength and truth. These are the blocks that form love. God ordained that parents should show and teach the following to their children:

i. **Kindness** to their children. To think of their children's needs and to be generous in meeting those needs.

ii. Show **humility** in front of their children. To model respect and a meek spirit, knowing that God says He will lift those who humble themselves up.

iii. Be **Selflessness**. A selfless parent seeks what is good for their child, even as far as improving their own lives so children can benefit.

iv. Be **Patient**. This is to teach a child that God sets all things in His time and season.

v. Show **Strength**. One has to have inner strength to hold to Godly principles in the face of adversity. A parent who embodies this allows their children to be the same.

vi. Live in **Truth**. Lying is seemingly a harmless exercise. But only the truth, all truth, brings us closer to God

These are the blocks that are together called love. When a child grows up receiving this love, it produces in their spirit an abundance of the same. We said in *Birthright* that it forms a cocoon of warmth enabling children to grow and mature into loving adults. This is unconditional love that is given without expecting anything in return.

A father would give strength and truth to a girl child. Fathers are heroes to their little girls. Their presence alone transfers strength and a sense of truth into their girl children. We idolise our fathers because they are who we belong to: we see them and we feel safe. And when Daddy comes to a daughter's level to cause her to smile, that is humility and kindness personified. Mothers are patient, their strength is gentle and their humility is confident, and that maternal instinct says you have to be kind to your own daughter.

A child who grows up in this environment will have strong fibres of love within themselves. They will know how to love themselves. This is a girl who, when the time is right, would never settle for less than the Love of God.

My prayer is that this book reaches people who do not come from ideal circumstances and environments, so that they might know that it is of the love of God that parents are supposed to pour into them. God is able to pour His love into you, even in situations where parents are unable to do so. Know that when love is given to you at a cost to you, that has ceased to be love: that is abuse. Love is free and cannot be bought or paid for. God knows His own and hears all prayers, even ones that are only a whisper spoken in darkness. He guarantees in His word that He is your strength when you are weak, and that He has already given you His Son Jesus to bear every burden that you might face. Jesus says we should pray by calling God our Father, who is in heaven.

9In this manner, therefore, pray

Our Father in heaven,
Hallowed be Your name.

MATTHEW 6: 9

God is our Father who is in heaven. We have so much amiss in our lives because we did not receive love as children; not enough to build a strong fibre of love in our lives, to build us up in love to equip us in readiness to love others.

This is the moment for you to know that God has bypassed all of the ills of your childhood. Choose to love Him and as a result your life will change daily to reflect the love of God in you.

Sharing in love

Loving anyone well requires that you love yourself. Please don't miss this point. You cannot presume to have a relationship with anyone if you do not first love yourself. You simply cannot give what you don't have.

At home with our siblings, we have relationships with our brothers and sisters when we are younger, that is not held together by our own love, but by the love our parents have for us. The reason relationships fall apart between siblings when parents die is that the bond of love can be removed by the death of a parent. Unless siblings forge their own bonds and find love for each other, the death of a parent can mean the breakdown of a family. In the same breath, you find people who are not related by blood forming deep connections that mimic family bonds, because of the love people can give to each other.

Love is a thread that connects human beings to each other. To have that special bond, you have to love yourself immensely, as God has loved you. That love in you will be what others receive and perceive as you loving them. The bible says that, when you begin to love others in this way, the love of God for you becomes more complete.

Dear friends, since God so loved us, we also ought to love one another. ¹²*No one has ever seen God; but if we love one another, God lives in us and his love is made complete in us.*

1 JOHN 4: 11

You begin to love others when you start to form your own relationships. A love between siblings is not guaranteed unless they choose to love one another. The choice to love our brothers and sisters should be automatic and not something one does at a certain age. We live in a society where brokenness in families can make loving your own siblings a difficult task; this is common when children are raised in broken homes.

You form friendships when you choose to love other girls in your own circle. The correct way to describe this is that friendships begin with mutual respect and admiration when two people like each other. We know of friends who have been together for years and love each other like sisters, because of the depth with which they choose to love each other. The bible teaches followers of Christ that **the way to live for God includes loving others deeply.**

[8] Above all, love each other deeply, because love covers a multitude of sins.
[9] Offer hospitality without crumbling. [10] Each of you should use whatever

> *gifts you have received to serve others, as faithful stewards of God's grace in its various forms.*
>
> 1 Peter 4: 8-10 NIV

The love that we should share with our friends should be meaningful, so that by how we love them they also receive the love of God. Even among brethren **we are instructed to love each other with a love that can transform lives** by covering a multitude of sins. We know that when our steps are ordered by the Lord, He can use us to be agents of change in the lives of those who were wronged or have been dealing with adversities. The bible says that, when we love others as God has loved us, it is that love that can cover a multitude of sins, correct past wrongs and bring people back to the Light of God. As we have already learned, the Love of God is a giving love. So, when we love others we have to be of service to them and not complain about giving more than we get in return. We receive from God and when we offer hospitality without crumbling, He in turn makes His love for us more complete.

For those of us who know how much God has loved us, **we are instructed to be genuine in the way we love others.** You know we sometimes give ourselves permission to fake our way through life and relationships, but the Word of God says to be truthful and Godly in the way you love others.

> *⁹Love must be sincere. Hate what is evil; cling to what is good. ¹⁰Be devoted to one another in love. Honour one another above yourselves.*
>
> *¹¹Never be lacking in zeal, but keep your spiritual fervor, serving the*

Lord. ⁱ²Be joyful in hope, patient in affliction, faithful in prayer. ¹³Share with the Lord's people who are in need. Practice hospitality.

ROMANS 12: 9-13

We are instructed to love others with a true heart, a heart that knows that all love is without cost to us because God gave His beloved Son, Jesus, to pay what it would have cost us. The way we love others should bring them honour as we humble ourselves in the task of servitude by being hospitable and addressing their needs.

The love that comes from God is love that supplies the needs of those who need more than we do. The love of God is able to replenish itself and therefore the more you give, the more you receive from our Heavenly Father. At times, when we do good to others, our good is repaid with wrong. **It is in love that we are able to forgive and continue to love those who have personally wronged us.** The scriptures gives us courage in giving love that forgives in Colossians 3: 12 – 14, which says:

> *¹²Therefore, as the elect of God, holy and beloved, put on tender mercies, kindness. Humility, meekness, longsuffering; ¹³bearing with one another, and forgiving one another, if anyone has a complaint against another; even as Christ forgave you, so you also must do. ¹⁴But above all these things put on love, which is the bond of perfection.*

When Jesus was teaching about love to His disciples, to those who had walked with Him the longest and were closest to Him, He said these words that are recorded in Luke 6: 27-32:

²⁷ "But to you who are listening I say: Love your enemies, do good to those who hate you, ²⁸bless those who curse you, pray for those who mistreat you. ²⁹If someone slaps you on the one cheek, turn to them the other also. If someone who asks your coat, do not withhold your shirt from them. ³⁰Give to everyone who asks you, and if anyone takes what belongs to you, do not demand it back. ³¹Do to others as you would have them do to you.

³² "If you love those who love you, what credit is that to you? Even sinners love those who, love them."

The scriptures above reflect the depth to which we should allow God's love to direct our lives. When we allow God to take full control of every aspect of our lives, in the full knowledge that His word is true and that He is the faithful God, we then are led to wholly experience kind, selfless, patient, strong and true love that comes from the heart of God. It is this love that shines through and is poured out to those who also need to know that God is Love. Jesus was teaching His inner group saying, "When we think about it, who needs love more than someone who has never experienced it?" It is easy to love lovable people, those who already know the love of God. But to bring real change in the world, we need to love those who are still in hatred and darkness and show them the way to God the Father. Jesus says that, if we want to take some credit in this love thing, we must go out and love in places where hatred reigns. Go to those who are discarded and teach them about God. Only then can we say we are love. He knew this would be hard for us to do, so He calls Himself love and gets us off the hook. All we have to do is tell the world about Jesus, our true Love, and He will do the rest.

The truth is, God is Love. He loves you immeasurably and His love endures forever. It runs from everlasting to everlasting. His message to us is simply that we must love Him, and that love will shine through to transform us and others.

Being found

The bible says, in Proverbs 18: 22, that:
^{22}He who finds a wife finds a good thing,
And obtains favour from the Lord

It used to be common practice that men were the ones who proposed to girls, and even then you would have him wait a couple of weeks on end while you decided whether you wanted to be his wife or not. This old-fashioned practice is actually biblical and founded in the Word of God. As a young lady, a young man who wants to love you and plan a life with you is supposed to find you. In matters of having a partner in life, you are supposed to be found, because you are a treasure that should be cherished and loved as God had loved us. Anyone who makes advances to forge a relationship with you must be serious and understand what it is that they want to achieve with you. Without that principle, then the relationship you have with this person is just to toy with you until they can find one with whom they will be serious.

We live in a world that permits relationships between young men and young women in their most sadistic and dysfunctional form. These relationships that are formed prematurely, before you know what love is, before you love yourself enough to love another, and before they also understand how to love you, will result in pain and load your life with undesirable grief and consequences that you can do without.

It is preferable to mature and have strides in your career and be on your journey to fulfil your purpose in life, and only then, with both feet on the ground and when you have direction, can you call yourself *a good thing, a wife to be found;* someone who can add value to someone's life and show the favour of God in their lives. A young lady who was designed by God to be in a relationship was Eve, who was said to be a *suitable helper*. As a young woman, dear Sis, your job in a relationship is to add favour to your partner. That is what makes the relationship different from any other you will have. God is love. That does not change, ever.

Having a partner in an intimate relationship is described as becoming one in the bible.

[24] Therefore a man shall leave his father and mother and be joined to his wife, and they shall become one flesh.

GENESIS 2: 24

[6] But from the beginning of the creation, God 'made them male and female.' [7] For this reason a man shall leave his father and mother and be joined to his wife, [8] and the two shall become one flesh; so then they are

no longer two, but one flesh, ⁹Therefore what God has joined together, let not man separate."

MARK 10: 6-9

God designed marriage between two individuals who are a man and woman to have them become one. This is a what a sexual relationship is. It is becoming one with your husband. When entering into that relationship, the foundation is in God, in the Love of God; your position is to show the favour of the Lord in your husband's life.

From his side (this is what you have to include on your list when you are praying for your future husband, that he must have these attributes):

He must first find you

He who finds a wife finds a good thing and obtains favour from the Lord.

PROVERBS 18:22

He must be a man who walks in the ways of God and seeks His righteousness

Do not be unequally yoked together with unbelievers. For what fellowship has righteousness with lawlessness? And what communion has light with darkness?

2 CORINTHIANS 6: 14

He must be someone who can love you as much as he loves himself

²⁵Husbands, love your wives, just as Christ also loved the church and gave Himself for her,
²⁸So husbands ought to love their own wives as their own bodies, he who loves his wife loves himself.

EPHESIANS 5: 25, 28

He must be able to toil the soil and provide for you

"Because you have heeded the voice of your wife, and have eaten from the tree of which I commanded you, saying 'You shall not eat of it':
"Cursed is the ground for your sake; In toil you shall eat of it all the days of your life.

GENESIS 3:17

Now Jacob loved Rachel; so he said, "I will serve seven years for Rachel your younger daughter."

GENESIS 29:18

He must be able to help you grow and mature

²²Wives, submit to your own husband, as to the Lord. ²³For the husband is the head of the wife, as also Christ is the head of the church; and He is the Saviour of the body.

EPHESIANS 5: 22 – 23

He must have room for growth and potential for more success and provide for his family

But if anyone does not provide for his own, and especially for those of his household, he has denied the faith and is worse than an unbeliever.

1 TIMOTHY 5:8

Now tell me, what is the aim and the point of having a boyfriend at a young age when you are not yet ready for marriage? Your body can only be protected by you and taken care of by you. Your body is the only real gift you have to give that will be with you forever. Protect yourself and don't indulge in things that do not honour you and honour who God is. When the time is right, your future husband will find you. Have faith in God and He will give you the desires of your heart. This is how the psalmist puts it:

¹Do not worry because of evildoers,
Nor be envious toward wrongdoers;
²For they will wither quickly like the grass,
And fade like the green herb.
³Trust (rely on and have confidence) in the Lord and do good;
Dwell in the land and feed (securely) on His faithfulness.
⁴Delight yourself in the Lord,
And He will give you the desires and petitions of your heart
⁵Commit your way to the Lord;
Trust in Him also and He will do it.
⁶He will make your righteousness (your pursuit of right standing with God) like the light,
And your judgement like (the shining of) the noonday (Sun).
⁷Be still before the Lord; wait patiently for Him and entrust yourself to Him;
Do not fret (whine, agonize) because of Him who prospers in his way,
Because of the man who carries out wicked schemes.

PSALM 37: 1-7 (AMP)

When it comes to making choices about any other thing we want to pursue in life, we ask for other people's opinions and get training and we wait to make sure that we are mature and responsible enough to handle the situation and be self-sufficient and successful. Marriage and starting a family is more permanent and more important than anything else you will ever do. Wait on the Lord and do not compare yourself with unbelievers. God is love and He has prepared that love for you; a man who will make it his mission to present you to God and to the world as glorious.

My dear sister, most of us got it wrong when it comes to relationships. You are hurting because of our mistakes. Our children have to spend weekends and holidays split between parents and have to make up their minds out of a string of men who Dad is. Our families are splashed on social media and are said to be *blended*. *Blended* and *complicated* do not appear anywhere in the bible as being what God designed for our lives.

We are people who make it work, so we pose and take selfies and we put on the cutest make-up and paste our dysfunctional life on social media as if that makes it all good. This is not the picture of happiness. This is the picture of brokenness and if you look more closely you will see the frowns we hide with care as we, for a second, acknowledge that things might have been different for you. There is nothing as hard to acknowledge, or as painful, as realising that the man you chose does not deserve you, that he is wrong in every way and that he will never be a covering for you in the eyes of God. This is something you want to realise before you even have a friendship with such a person because, once married, biblically you are stuck with them.

> *[16] "For the Lord God of Israel says that He hates divorce,*
> *For it covers one's garment with violence"*
> *Says the Lord of hosts.*
> *"Therefore take heed to your spirit,*
> *That you do not deal treacherously."*
>
> MALACHI 2:16

Breaking up a family brings violence; there is nothing like a happy divorce. Breaking up a family, even the ones that you put yourselves in by staying with a man and starting a family before marriage, *masihlalisane*, brings violence and hurt and pain, especially to the lives of the innocent children.

Dear Sis, love is when you obey God and walk in His ways. Love is when you seek His face and He pours into you and you feel His love that overflows in your life. When you have the love of the Father, you can stand knowing that you can love yourself fully and can love others as much. For the man who is to marry you, you are to become one with him in God. Let him do the work of loving, and you submit to him and add favour in his life.

Let us pray.

> Dear God. Thank you for loving me. Amen

Stepping Out

GROWING UP, FROM EARLY ON parents introduce "the reward system", where a child is rewarded for being good and punished for being bad, as well as being rewarded for certain achievements and punished for failing in certain areas. This is a principle that is ingrained in our minds: that being good and attaining accolades is rewarded and being bad and failure is punishable. Self-determination is when each individual defines for themselves what being good means and which accolades one should strive for. Self-determination functions on defining for oneself the limit in the sky and what it would take to get there.

We have seen this poster that describes a generation of rich millennials born to parents who were themselves poor. The poster shows a pampered child who is brought up wanting for nothing, yet the children are incapable of crafting careers and providing for themselves what their previously disadvantaged parents were able to. This is what a lack of self-determination produces: a dormancy of inner drive to be bigger and better than what you presently are.

In other circumstances we have seen siblings grow up in the same household and provided with the same opportunity, but one will grow up to be successful and the other becomes unable to leave their family home. What sets them apart, in the absence of confounding factors, is self-determination.

Self-determination is an inner drive and a voice that continually asks the questions: **Do you have a destination for your dreams? Do you have an instrument to transform your dreams into realities?** Are you maturing into someone who will be useful in the future? Do you have a role model who can demonstrate for you what you are trying to become?

The root of the problem

Most of the time, if not all the time, parents can only take you up to the levels they know. **You will become that which you were told you will become,** either by parents speaking into your life and coaching you in how to be or by being surrounded by role models who demonstrate and live out your possibilities. If your parent is not able to expand their own vision of who you are, then they are not going to be instrumental in seeing you become fully who you are destined to be. A parent who cannot stretch margins of possibility for themselves would find it impossible to do that for another human being.

It is a tragic reality that often the lessons learned by our parents from painful experiences and memories of their past can shock them so severely that it becomes impossible to hope for more in life, be it for themselves or for you.

Overcoming the obstacle

My dear sister, you are everything your intuition tells you that you are. When those who are meant to guide you into becoming the best you will be are unable to do so for whatever reasons, know this: God, in His infinite power, has placed in our being a knowing that we are bigger than our circumstances and environments. Self-determination is that willingness to do what it takes to access the inner you and become the woman who lives to honour God.

Self-determination lives and is nourished by hope. You have to keep hope alive, no matter how dim the light might become. You have to keep hoping that tomorrow is writing a different chapter than the one you see today and each day be sensitive to opportunities to do what it takes.

Many people have taken an opportunity to take credit in "how I turned out". Some credit is well deserved, some... not so much. Like most black children, I was raised by a village, but the person who actually raised me was my uncle, *Mbiba*, whose voice I still hear in my head even today. He was a man of many simplicities in quantity and immense complexities in thought and quality.

The one thing he taught me is to have no fear in taking the next step. So, my life has been a series of taking one step at a time and then looking forward to see what the next step will be without fear and doubt. Although we were poorer than most, he would always impress on my then impressionable mind that I am as capable as any human being, if not more capable because my hunger and desire was deeper than most. Each day growing up, he would point out that I still had two hands, two feet and a brain that absorbs and processes information faster than average, and he would ask what I intended to do with it. I am blessed that I had *Mbiba* growing up. He was a thinker of note and he knew how to paint big horizons and paths that lead to them.

Self-determination is lost without the ability to conceptualise tomorrow. It is the vehicle that girls who are positioned like I was, way below the margin of poverty, ride to have access to a different reality. It is not blind ambition, which is a haphazard way of living life and leads one astray. Self-determination is harvested: someone who is bigger than yourself, who knows better than you do, who has been there and done that should call it up in you.

People always point to someone who saw in them what they couldn't see while still young: a parent, a teacher, an older sibling, a neighbour, a God-sent messenger who ignites the drive and the determination within. Even though it is harvested, it remains self because, although it is ignited, it solely depends on you what happens next. You have to believe in the reality of a different existence from where you are and will your mind to do all it takes to get there. The sky, as they say, is the limit. Self-determination allows you to keep moving forward to higher goals and bigger milestones, depending on how high you are willing to reach.

The bible, in the book of Ruth, relates the story of a poor widow called Naomi, whose two sons had also passed away. Naomi was now poverty stricken in a foreign country called Moab and left with the responsibility of being a mother-in-law to her two daughters-in-law who were now also widows. The names of the daughters-in-law are

Ruth and Orpah. The bible says Naomi decided for herself that she would go back to her place of origin, which was Bethlehem in Judah. She gave her young daughters-in-law permission to return to their families and start life afresh, instead of living as widows at such a young age. The book is called Ruth, because it relates further the story of how Ruth, unlike Orpah, was determined within herself to be with Naomi.

In Chapter One, the narrative reads that Ruth saw a different reality for herself by sticking with Naomi and going with her to Bethlehem. The reality she saw for herself was limitless. She asserts:

For wherever you go, I will go; and wherever you lodge, I will lodge. Your people shall be my people and, and your God, my God.

Ruth 1: 16b

Self-determination is harvested. Naomi had seen potential in Ruth and called it out by telling her to go and seize the opportunity to have a full life despite both of them losing husbands and being left in poverty. In this scenario, Naomi had lived her life. She had been a wife, a mother, had lived in riches and opportunity and now lived in poverty and in mourning for her husband and sons. She had been so much further than where Ruth was, and she knew and had lived a different reality to the one in which they presently found themselves. She is a God-sent messenger for Ruth in affirming to Ruth that her end of days will not be counted in sorrow and poverty; that she can change her life and reality.

God is the Creator and He sets everything in order to show His glory in all His creation. He always provides a platform for a new leap and new heights. When God has sent someone to call greatness in you, it does not become difficult to see God at the end of your journey. The person will be God-sent, used by God and will point you in a direction that can only lead to God. It is, in fact, intrinsically God who calls out that which He put in you.

Are you in a place in life where you are ready to move along in the journey of life? Seek God and His message will be clear.

Self-determination is ignited. When Ruth heard from Naomi that she could still find a husband who could provide for herself and that she could have a family, her vision of who she was changed. She says to Naomi that she will have a home (lodging), she will have a family (her people) and that she will have God on their side.

Self-determination has a clear voice and is logical in reasoning. Realising it is like turning on an engine that sets into motion the reality of the truth about yourself that lies within. The pinnacle of Ruth's realisation is that she will have God on her side and will have a relationship with Him. Ruth was probably taught by her in laws who God was, because Ruth was a Moabite and originally a pagan. God revealed Himself to be above all other gods that she might have known in her native Moab. Imagine a prophecy in your life that says, walk the journey and the pinnacle of your existence will be having God Almighty as your God. Receive in reality that God says He will be found by those who seek Him and He will become your Father when you ask Him to be. And, like Ruth, you will realise that He is above all other deities and beings you might have known before.

When you hear the voice of God calling you to greatness, light up, switch your engines on and be fully ignited to live your life in your highest level existence.

Self-determination lives in hope. Ruth hoped with all her might that going to Bethlehem with Naomi would not be the beginning of the end for them, but a new beginning to a better future.

The book further narrates in its four chapters that Naomi continued to point out to Ruth which steps to take until they were both living in abundance, and Ruth was married and had a family of her own.

While self-determination is a driving force to tomorrow, hope is today. Hope makes a difference immediately and doesn't depend on a span of time passing, nor any present conditions to change before it makes a change in your life. Hope knows to see bigger, better and more in every situation. Hope speaks of what God can do, starting from where you are until His complete will is done. Self-determination lives in hope. While we are self-determined and work to get there, we move in hope that each step brings us closer to God and His will in our lives will come to pass. Self-determination is a gift to each and every one of us, that enables us to fill every space, every pocket, and every avenue of our lives.

Self-determination requires that you resolve to do whatever it takes. In the bible story that we are narrating, we see Ruth taking a drastic decision to venture with her mother-in-law to a country and place that she has never been to. That is a tough decision for anyone to make. We see in the same breath Orpah deciding to stay in Moab and her story is lost to the biblical audience. Ruth did not know by any stretch of imagination what the next thing in her life would be. We assume all she had was hope for a new day. The women had heard (Ruth 1:6) that in Bethlehem of Judah there was plenty of food, instead of the famine that was in Moab. In the land of plenty, there is hope that there will be enough to pass along.

Resolving to do what it takes is the willingness to take the first step despite what things might look like. This is not done blindly, but one stays in the hope that God, Who is faithful, will see us through.

Doing what it takes includes what might be called just pure stubbornness outside the church, but it is actually FAITH. Faith is moving forward at a steady pace, and pushing through, and expecting positive results, and not giving up, and trusting that all you do will bring you to what you were meant to be. Faith dispels fear and doubt and gives you knowledge that God will fill in all the gaps and pay all the debts and redeem the time you put in, because He is God. Faith is moving, pressing in and trusting that, in a parallel dimension, God is working all things for your good.

Doing what it takes means a willingness to listen and be taught. In this Old Testament book we see that Ruth took every instruction and advice that Naomi had to give her.

Doing what it takes means having the discipline to work hard, to be honest and being trustworthy. We live in an era where rules are bent and changed to suit those who are in power at the time. This does not in any way improve your lives or honour God. What you are becoming should at all times be that which gives God glory. Ruth worked in the fields of one of Naomi's rich relatives called Boaz. She didn't offend the workers in the field, but always stayed a little behind, to submit to their authority and protocols. This is how you work, without cutting corners or expecting ungodly benefits, but accepting what is due to you and trusting God to cause a divine increase to the work of your hands.

Doing what it takes means that we have come to understand and appreciate the meaning and value of time. Only God can give and only God can take time away. We have devised means of replacing time or redeeming time with money. If we can't employ time to do something and perform a task, we pay someone to do it. Yet, in truth, we cannot buy time. It is a person who is becoming what they were meant to be who understands how to use time effectively. Time well spent is an investment and what you do in any given moment can either be rewarding or be costly to you. How best to use your time can only be received by being connected to God, the One who ordained the number of days by calling the first day to the second and resting on the seventh day.

We all have time as a free gift. What we choose to do with the time we have is more valuable than any future investments we might acquire. Whatever you spent most of your time doing, is what will show up as fruits of your labour in your life over and over again. Use your time to better yourself and to position yourself so that, when an opportunity is presented to you, you are found ready and prepared.

Naomi, as she mentors Ruth, knows this truth. Naomi knows that God has a time for all moments of our life, both good and bad, and in Him there is the ultimate fullness of joy and completion of what we are for His purpose (see Ruth 1: 21-22 and Ruth 4: 14).

Dear Sis, it has always been up to you to become what you were meant to be. It has always been within your power. Each day you wake up in new hope and vast possibilities. The determination within is a fire from God to keep you moving, milestone to milestone. It might be difficult to hear this if you face extreme poverty and dire hardship. Your dreams don't have to be overwhelming to begin with; your vision is allowed to be only where you place your next step, and then the next. In retrospect you will realise that the proverb that says "A journey of a thousand miles starts with one little step" is absolutely true. Sometimes the seemingly insurmountable number of difficulties ahead of us can pull us down and block our imaginations, but consider that all you have to do is:

- Pass well academically, put the effort in and give it your all
- Fill in an application form for a bursary or scholarship or get a part-time job
- Set rules for yourself and respect them
- Identify and stay away from distractions and bad influences
- Then try your absolute best every time and learn from every situation
- Ask for help
- Reward yourself for small victories
- And then do it again, and again

Before you know it, you are more of who you are becoming than who you were.

Self-determination speaks of your willingness to go through the process of change, embracing it fully and being all you can be, for yourself and for your people, to the glory of God.

Let us pray.

> Dear Lord God, You are the creator of all things and the giver of life. In ourselves we do not know what gifts we have, but in you, Father, we have all that we seek. Order my steps and bring me to Your will. Be my God and be my King. Guide and lead me to a place that is higher than my circumstances, for the glory of Your name. Amen.

Living, Not Surviving

WE BELIEVE THAT LIFE MUST be nice. "Nice" is a word that the dictionary defines to be synonymous with enjoyable, pleasant, satisfying, acceptable, agreeable, good, and so on. For a child who is born *disadvantaged*, "nice" is a very obscure idea. Being born into a family that is at any one point struggling to make ends meet, while numbing the pain and weight of the hardship and struggle by any means possible, can distort the picture of what joy and pleasure would look like. We grow up seeing adults drink themselves to a stupor every weekend and freely indulge in behaviours that do not honour God, for the sake of escaping reality, relaxing, giving themselves a break from the hardness of life, self-reward, or simply because that is how they live their lives and we come to understand this as how to live life in joy and pleasure; we understand this as what a "nice" life looks like, even though this is not the entire truth.

I am a Christian. I have been one for a really long time and so my idea of what fun should be is in the far extreme and biased towards singing hymns and making "clean" jokes. I am also now older and mature and I can have a nice time in silence while standing absolutely still. I am also a self-confessed introvert, so when it comes to a "nice" time, I personally think there is nothing wrong with a good book or a thought-provoking movie that also happens to have lots of cheerful music, sunny colours and a happily ever after. That is my "nice time".

Both of the above are extremes and neither is the ideal script for anyone's life. The reality of life is that time is presented to us in a twenty-four-hour span, which we can use to be productive and to sleep. The days are packed into weeks and the weeks into months and months into years. **Living life requires that you use the packaged moments to be useful (putting something in), to be productive (gain profit) and to be helpful (sharing the rewards).**

No matter what popular belief might be, this you have to do on your own: you have to be useful, productive and helpful, yourself. In your own life and with the things you do, and the way you do them, you should live a life that brings you immense joy, satisfaction, delight and peace. Life has to be "nice" every day. The twenty-four hours should be filled with light and contentment in themselves, because **joy is not a future goal, it is a daily gift.** Living life means waking up daily and declaring that today, with all it brings, is worth living.

One might think that this is an easy concept only when life is good and everything is set for success. For most of us who are born poor and disadvantaged, we are automatically wired to think that life is not set for success and that joy is undermined and buried in pain and struggle. We unconsciously think that joy is only for the elite and so a "nice time" is only had on a weekend schedule, in a reality that is distorted and falsified by a numb mind.

The things that are scheduled for weekends as "nice time", where we see people drowning in alcohol and drugs and partying and behaving badly, are not in anyway the end game. No one will ever give you credit for the number of parties you attended, and your body will display every abuse you bestowed on it. There are people with no dreams, no goals and no imagination; they do not dare venture out for fear of failure. These people are genuinely not trying to become anything, they are not trying to build anything and are not trying to change anything. They want to live just to be drunk another day and party another day. They might even be delusional by calling this *a phase of life*, but no *phase of life* lasts for a decade or two. When you see someone do something long enough without intention or efforts to achieve anything else and be something else, they are actually living their life at that level. They might call it *nice*, but the question is: is it the level at which you want to exist? Are you brave enough to rise to where you are meant to be?

We live in a world where we have a number of theories and philosophies to explain our existence and to make sense of who, what and why we are. We also have a number of institutions of thought to justify our failures and our fears. I acknowledge all of them, whatever they might be. I recognise the past and the marks it left on us as a society, as a people and as individuals. Yet, today is here despite all of that. The last twenty-four hours came and went and the next has presented itself. Today, in the now, in this moment, what are you doing that exhibits who, what and why you are here?

Time flows and moments overlap. There is no clear margin where we are done with that and we pause, debrief, allow a lapse in the continuum and then start again. Things just keep moving, whether we move with them or not. Because of this continuum, I pray that the people raising you recognised a moment when life stopped being about them and loved you enough to make it about you as they taught you the tools of living a joyous and content life, full of light and hope. If this happened for you, you are blessed and highly favoured. If not, do not worry. The reason you are reading this book is because of this moment; right now and here, God has decided that your time has come to live life in full and not be overshadowed by the past.

1. Being useful

This is how my generation grew up: as soon as our hands could reach and our feet became steady, we began to learn to do chores. Often these were imposed on us and most of us resisted initially. When I was growing up, like most of my peers, I wasn't given a choice as to whether I wanted to do the chores or not. They had to be done. Doing chores didn't (and I hope still doesn't) exempt one from doing academic projects and school work. The rule was that the older you get, the more the responsibility that was piled on you, both at home and at school. As a child, the concept of having to do things for yourself and others is difficult to understand and chores and other activities that are not of one's choosing might be difficult to accept as part of what living life in joy is. The actual chores were hard labour because of our lack of basic necessities, but they were part of normal life. We grew up then in a life style that taught us that you have to work hard to get something in return.

Because of this fact – that we had to do hard labour as chores as well as balance school work and time with friends – we don't demand that you do chores as much. We can also afford *bo-ausi*, servants and maids and helpers and so on, so chores are not a necessary skill that you as young ladies growing up have to learn. At times, we overstep and complain about the volume of school work you bring home. The life style that you have been set up in as the younger generation might be one that gives an impression and a message that says that you don't have to work hard to achieve, but you have to be provided for in order to have, and that work is not fulfilling and joyous.

We learned to be useful while we were very young. We grew up knowing that we have to put something in to get something out. We grew up in a transitional era, where change was much accelerated and not easily predictable. Our mothers, however, grew up in an era where their parents had land and productivity and things were more stable and predictable. In their time, you tilled the soil, grew your crop, got a good harvest and provided for your family. When the shift came, our parents had to learn from the inventors of machines and company owners; and they had to adapt when the meaning of being useful changed. The meaning of being useful will continue to change, but you have to position yourself to be of use.

We can't have you grow up with a false belief that, for you to own anything and achieve anything, you have to be provided for or that success and ownership of anything are put into your lap without any effort on your part. We cannot have you grow up believing that, without your being provided for, life is sad. Although you are millennials, you still have to be useful.

To learn to be useful simply means learning to find joy in putting in the effort, in showing up daily, in learning new skills and in doing your best. We don't want you to be deep in hard labour that borders on child abuse; we don't want you to be walking behind machine makers and company owners all your life; but we do want you to find joy when your hands take hold of your destiny.

You were made and were meant to be able to contribute to society and you were made to fully survive your lifespan. You were given an intellect that can come up with new innovations and new ideas. Being a millennial means that you are closer than I am to the pulse of creativity; therefore be useful. You were equipped with strength and power that can be augmented by technology to do more than we ever could; therefore move what needs shifting to be of use. You are here now, where freedom is celebrated. There is freedom of speech, expression, movement, association, religion, sexuality – there is a freedom of everything under the sun. Use this freedom to release your inhibitions and reach out to touch and taste a truly successful life. Take the freedom to reach new heights and new levels.

When you are useful in serving others, and invariably observing from those who have done it before, you learn a new skill, but you also form relationships with people. You make friendships and make bonds that are also worthy and will carry you further in life in the absence of money. Being useful exposes you to humanity, so that you learn people's characters and it makes you sensitive to human needs. It allows you to learn from others how to think and process information. Being among people in society allows you to learn human behaviour passively, see their mistakes and learn from them.

It allows you to see people who experience real joy and real love and, when you are out among people being useful, you can feel your heart warm up and incline you to certain paths, pointing in the direction in which you should go. When you put yourself out there to be useful you learn not only vocational skills, but you learn about life in all its avenues, and you see the world and can identify your place in it.

Go with joy. Choose a place where there is truth and light and people break into song for no reason. Go towards a vocation that you feel right at home in, as if you have been doing it forever. Choose a place where you are at peace, no matter what the conditions are; serve where your whole being can be applied and you are the best you can be. When you allow yourself to serve like that, and the place calls out the best in you, you will in turn attract the right people into your life: people who will see you for who you are and honour you for your service. Some lessons in life are free and serving others is how you are schooled by life.

My dear sister, curl your lips up and form a smile, throw your head back and burst out in laughter. LIVE! No one is confining you to the township you live in, no one is confining you to a certain career choice, and no one is confining you to any place or space you don't want to be in. LIVE. If, when you open your eyes, you don't like what you see, use this twenty-four hours to make a plan on how to get out of there. This twenty-four hours will flow into the next and become a week. This week will flow into the next and become a month, these months will turn into years; and these years could be the journey you travelled to be useful. In that given time, be useful. Plant your youthful energy and efforts as an investment and let life teach you success.

The bible says, in Ephesians 5: 15 – 17 (AMP):

[15] Therefore see that you walk carefully (living life with honour, purpose, and courage; shunning those who tolerate and enable evil), not as the unwise, but as wise (sensible, intelligent, discerning people), [16] making the very most of your time (on earth, recognizing and taking advantage of each opportunity and using it with wisdom and diligence), because the days are (filled with) evil. [17] Therefore do not be foolish and thoughtless, but understand and firmly grasp what the will of the Lord is.

There are people who have always known what they were to become when they are adults. From early on they had the discipline and the mentorship to achieve their set goals expediently. Whatever difficulties and challenges might crop up, you are able to face them head on when the goal is clear. Each challenge, even ones that take several attempts to overcome, is seen as a lesson to teach and equip you to get to your goals. Knowing where you are going allows you to put in more effort and be of more use in that area. It allows you to focus more on your goals and give less attention to other things that will not build you up. When you have no idea whom you are becoming earlier in life, you spend a lot of time *finding yourself*. You end up surviving not only the past, but also the mistakes you cultivate when living a life that has no direction. Living life in survival mode reduces your usefulness and it steals your opportunity to actually live intentionally with a clear view of the choices you are making rather than having to cope with what you happen to have.

Choosing to be useful propels you to move to a place where your life is made fuller and more complete when you learn and serve others.

Let me make an extreme example. If you knew at the age of ten that you were called to be a preacher of the Word of God, would you be found in bars and shebeens, or in church and non-profit organisations sharing the gospel? If you were convinced that you are a preacher of God's Word, who is sent to those who are in such places to bring them to the Lord, would you be of use in a shebeen before or after you had learned everything there is to learn about God and the ministry of Jesus Christ? Say indeed you are a preacher of the Word. Would hanging around shebeens and bars before being taught prepare you to be useful in anyway?

Being useful means acquiring the discipline to put in an effort to learn, showing up to receive the lessons, allowing moments to transform and teach you how to be what you were meant to be and, while you take hold of it, doing your best. This understanding and knowledge should free your mind from the illusion that change requires no effort. You should be freed from thinking that having to work hard is being oppressed and associated with sadness. Find joy in your daily vocation.

A person who is inclined to work in law enforcement will not wreck their lives building a CV that does not speak of his character and trustworthiness. Such a person might move towards leadership ventures and organisations that have justice in their structural make up. When you avail yourself and find immense joy in the beginning of your journey, serving others and learning along the way; that joy would light a career path that would be fulfilling and enriching.

Being useful, embracing the hard work and applying your whole being to serving others is the first step in living life intentionally. Lessons that are learned on such a journey enable you to make your own conscious choices in life and not live life by mishap and default.

2. Being productive

Young people grow up to become adults and move out of their parents' homes to forge a life of their own. On the other hand, parents grow older, retire and eventually depend in their kids to support them in one way or another. When kids don't support their elderly parents, it is a sign of a broken paradigm, when adult children do not grow up to be independent, it is a sign of paradigm dysfunction. Eventually, each human being has to show something they have made of themselves.

The continuum of life is not only confined to time but to who we are as people. In a family we look alike, we share the same genetic code, we behave the same way, and we tend to have a similar level of achievements when we are growing up together. We have noted that when someone lifts up the standard and inspires the next generation in a family or in any societal group, the proceeding generation achieves more than what their predecessors could. It is magical, almost unheard of, for one person to jump leaps and bounds of achievement stages in either direction, to show a huge amount of change positively or negatively.

The continuum generally flows to show progressive change throughout generations and would be something like a move from being a disadvantaged group to being people who hold down jobs and are well employed; from being an employee to college graduate, from a college graduate to multiple university degrees, to post graduate qualifications, to self-employed, to company owner. Of course, there are other parallels that show a flow of change, a shift of paradigm as families progress through time. There are also exceptions to the rule where a person who comes from almost nothing becomes a billionaire in a lifetime, in a span of one generation: take Oprah Winfrey for example as the extreme exception.

The point, however, is that there is usually a continuum. What I have learned, what I know, what I am, I am passing to you so that you do not have to start at the point of nought (*zero*). This is how changes are made. My dear sister, be productive, make sure there is something to show for the work you put in. Have something that you can give to another human being and contribute to the universe. When you were younger and willing yourself to be useful and you were largely serving others, that was preparation for you to be able to profit from the universe, from others and to live from the fruits produced by your work. When we live a life that is born out of the joy of serving others, the Lord lights up our path and prepares a heavenly reward by living life where our careers are not a means to an end but a ministry in their own right. Living a life by fully applying yourself and being fully who you are is how we should truly live; in joy to build and effect change for the glory of God.

In the bible, in the book of Colossians 3: 23-24, Paul teaches concerning serving others that:

[23] whatever you do, do it heartily, as to the Lord and not to men, [24] knowing that from the Lord you will receive the reward of the inheritance; for you serve the Lord Christ.

We all emerge from somewhere, yet we cannot set our minds by where we are from, only by where we are going. Ahead is all hope and all possibilities. If the continuum of life flows through time and through people, then you have to believe this as the truth to change your paradigm and set your mind on things ahead and not on the past.

- What I have learned is that productivity does not have to be unique but that it is by nature a commodity that is transferable and beneficial
- What I know is that corrupted seeds produce undesirable fruits. This means we have to set our minds to learn from yesterday, forgive all of it and only remember what was good and worthy about it. Sow the seed for the next harvest in joy and peace. Giving ourselves to more joy and more peace leads to goodness and just rewards.
- What my peers and I are, are achievers. We landed on our feet. We made it. We give you permission to stand on our shoulders, the giants that we are, as we have stood on the shoulders of others. Don't fall. Rise. That means that we have fought every mentionable challenge that threatened to belittle

us or at least have shone spotlights on them. Now just RISE. Call on us as older sisters and we will help.

Lack of productivity is brokenness and bankruptcy
We live in a world where the common belief is that we have to take and consume. Taking and consuming leads to bankruptcy of the spirit. People who live from pay check to pay check and one weekend adventure to another, and have not set their minds to being productive, are bankrupt in spirit. They live life in fatigue, in exhaustion and are depressed all the time. When one lives life in the negative, on the back foot and in bankruptcy, one has to find alternative means to cope. Unfortunately, with a bankrupt spirit, the means to cope also includes accepting the negative, broken, bankrupt reality as the norm.

A broken and bankrupt existence easily leads to dependency on substances, including alcohol, drugs, sex and sexual immorality and other obsessive and ill behaviours. When something is labelled as being "normal" by yourself, even when it is not productive, not contributing anything to building you up, no matter who says otherwise, you would never think to change it. Having a bankrupt, broken spirit will eventually compromise your character. Who you become will attract people around you who can relate to your condition. That means that none among the fallen can rise to be better than they were before because, unfortunately, there is comfort in numbers.

In this manner, you are set to live life at the lowest possible level of existence and, instead of being positioned to choose, to be more, and to find peace and light, you are preoccupied with staying on the surface, surviving instead of living. A broken, bankrupt existence is not living life. The way to life is by receiving healing from the brokenness; by being filled up with goodness and light, so that the joy within can be seen. Only a person who has been healed from the brokenness of yesterday can start to be productive.

Economists put it simply that, when you start a job, make it a habit to use only 80% of your salary and keep 20% to invest in a future and for charitable deeds. It sounds very straight forward, right? I know, the problem that we all have is that we start life at a negative anyhow, with student loans, and that dreaded *black tax*, and the credit card and store card debts we took when were young and ignorant, and then we were chasing our tails in exhaustion trying to play catch up. We take this loan to pay the other loan while we also have to keep up with the *Kumalos*. Then we read a book about saving 20% and we realise that we are back footed and we become even more stressed and overwhelmed and we are depressed and put it out on social media that depression is for real and yet, nothing has changed. We are still in bankruptcy of spirit, broken and unproductive.

But, if we learned to be useful, we would realise that we have much more than we think. We have human resources around us and we have relationships and people who care. We can afford to lean on each other and make the strides required for the healing process to fully take its course. We can start building by simply deciding to stop rubbishing everything we have. We can save the 20% of what we have, not only in monetary terms, but you can give 20% of your time to others, 20% of your time to yourself wholly, 20% of your joy and laughter shared, another percentage in hard work and yet another in learning and improving.

Healing is a process and it can start as soon as you decide to be different from yesterday. God is the Chief Physician to heal the spirits of men. He can heal us and surround us with things and people that bring us closer to Him. He can replace the negativity with an overflow of abundance. He can lead us down paths that walking on will never be overwhelming and impossible. God will always surround us with people who make our journey lighter, more peaceful and full of joy. Receive healing from God and begin to see the fruit of His Spirit in every walk of your life.

Being productive means to set your mind to live life on the positive, in the fullness of Spirit, from a place of overflow and abundance and not from the brokenness we were accustomed to.

Let me show you how to set your mind to live a productive life.

My late paternal grandmother, *Mme*, who was born in early 1900, in a small town outside Kimberly, was a giant we all stand on today. She was a very intelligent woman and she was privileged to achieve a skill to write and read and teach at a primary school. She was a pastor's wife, but my grandfather died early in their married life and left her with six children and in poverty. She decided that what she'd learned, what she knew and what she was, was enough to live a productive life and to compel her children to do the same. She decided before I was born that she was going to be alright somehow, and that she would not live in poverty all her life. So she pushed all her kids to laugh and be happy, even in the face of poverty. She taught them that God is all knowing and has a plan and therefore there is no need to live life in mourning and sadness. She had faith and prayed her way out of dire situations. She instilled hope and a joyful spirit in their hearts and they could confront the world with bold spirits and positive attitude, instead of negativity and defeat.

The story is told that she would tell them stories about how great and magnificent they were and what important people they would become. She would insist that they maintain a high level of personal hygiene and that they should show up on time every time with a good attitude and that they should never complain and moan about their poverty. She made them love life and dream of ample possibilities for their lives.

Most of my uncles and aunts were successful in their own right. My father was beat by *black tax*, being the first born and taking up the role of "the provider" and "father-figure" in the shoes of his late father. My mother, also a *Kimberlite*, was not like my grandmother. She had come from a place of relative comfort and was somewhat sheltered in her upbringing. She was not yet a fighter in spirit but, after being mentored by *Mme* and learning from her, my mother adopted a victor's spirit as well.

She married a man who had too much to carry, both personally and through his calling, and who was burdened. My mother gave everything she had to my father as a good wife to help him raise the extended family and his own family.

Both my parents were spread too thin and raised us (their own children) from a bankruptcy of spirit. We should have been messed up nice and good – in fact, we were messed up nice and good, as are most children who are raised by parents who are depleted, stretched too thin and filling too many roles. The system of brokenness outside in society and the frame of brokenness within the home can cause anyone to go mad and perpetuate the depletion within that leads to clinical depression.

Mme was given grace to live until her calling was done. She was able to impart into her grandchildren the same drive that she raised her children with. She stood as someone who could testify to the fact that, as long as you can take some of the good in you and transfer it to another, when you plant that goodness in joy and peace, it faithfully crops to produce good fruit, so that the wars that have been won do not have to be fought again. She allowed us to stand on her shoulders and see further. She showed us what being able to channel your life to be productive is like.

Mbiba was raised well by *Mme* and when she passed on, *Mbiba* took over from where *Mme* had left off in my upbringing. He made it clear for me that being productive for me, and for each and every person, is what and how we choose for it (productivity) to be. Being productive is being able to harvest from the seeds you planted for your life by being of use. Being productive is living a life that gives you joy and honours God. Living in this way means that what you do is not shameful and honours who, what and why you were born.

I know that some of you were denied the blessing of having *Mme* and *Mbiba* in your lives, denied by so much and so many, raised as orphans, raised in abuse, raised in dire circumstances. So I stand to tell you this because I know it to be the truth: you can stand on our shoulders and RISE. Prices were paid on your behalf, sacrifices were made on your behalf. Your laughter and joy, despite everything that might still exist, is confirmation that you are strong and you are healing and that you are ready to live a life that is profitable to you and your family. Let your labour that is sown in hope and love prove profitable on your behalf. The bible puts it this way:

> *God is not unjust, He will not forget your work and the love you have shown Him as you have helped His people and continue to help them.*
>
> HEBREWS 6: 10 NIV

It is a blessing when one is able to find joy in what one does and how one lives and with whom one shares time and life. But at times we do what we have to do while we work our way to what we know we were called to do. God is not deterred by life circumstances and situations. Our only duty when it comes to living life consciously and not just surviving the circumstances of our existence is to be sure to honour God through it all. Being purposefully productive is living in the knowledge that God is able to move every piece of creation as one moves chess pieces. He is the One who holds all things and wills all things to pass and, even through hiccups and challenges, joy will be found in Him. We have to pray our way through and hope our way through and be led by His Spirit through it all. When the Spirit of the Lord is leading, we are blessed to have His joy guide our steps.

David worships the Lord in the book of Psalms when he realises the goodness of the Lord in his life and that he was able to live a life that pleases the Lord despite all the battles he fought, all the hardship by persecution and illness. He comes to a point in life where he is able to build a magnificent home for himself and his family and, in thanking the Lord, he says;

> [1] *I will extol You, O Lord, for You have lifted me up,*
> *And have not let my foes rejoice over me.*
> [2] *O Lord my God, I cried out to You,*
> *And You healed me.*
> [3] *O Lord, You brought my soul up from the grave;*
> *You have kept me alive, that I should not go down to the pit.*
> [4] *Sing praise to the Lord, you saints of His,*
> *And give thanks at the remembrance of His holy name.*
> [5] *For His anger is but for a moment,*
> *His favour is for life*
> *Weeping may endure for a night,*
> *But joy comes in the morning.*

The above verses, written in Psalm 30, confirm that God can lift us up from any depth, including from the point of death. God can heal all our past pain. We might cry for a while but joy will come in the morning. Being productive means you know that joy has come and that you are now profitable in life, that your life is pleasing in the eyes of God and that, through what you do, through how you choose to live, by the people that surround you, you can bring glory to the kingdom of God. Through how you choose to live your life, your family can profit and enjoy the goodness of the living God. The favour of the Lord lasts for a life time.

Every seed that has been planted eventually grows up for consumption, unless the seed was poisonous to begin with. Every genuine effort you make will pay off. This is true. Sow in the joy of the Lord and be led by His Spirit to live the life that He has planned for you.

3. Being helpful

You have not lived a complete cycle of life if you have not been helpful. Not everyone knows the absolute truth. The truth is that life is not a series of moving from one failure to another, or even finding ways to sabotage yourself and others. Holding on to what does not work for the sake of holding on is not living consciously. Be helpful and be willing to pass on what you have, so that others can find the same light that you have found. In other words, build a legacy.

The reason we find it hard when someone dies when they are too young is because we believe that it takes time for anyone to fully understand life and to become productive enough to let that profitability speak for who, what and why they were here. We are left with questions and confusion when a life was lived and, in a few decades, is gone without having had any clarity as to what their purpose was.

When a young successful person dies, we take comfort in saying that *they had lived*, even though we might mourn what else they could have done and become. The reaction to a young, successful person dying implies that we have seen some of their talent and gifts and they shared that with us.

When old people die, we grieve, but under our breath we say, *they had lived*, or that *they have gone to rest*, meaning that they have worked hard and have shared their lives. A large crowd is expected at a burial ceremony of someone who had shared life with more people, while only a handful show up at a beggar's funeral.

Legacy is built one day at a time, one person at a time, from moment to moment. When you are in the company of others, what are you imparting to them? Reputations follow us and the impact you strive to make is registered by God, who sees all your works. Being helpful involves sharing your gift and talents with others, lifting each other up and moving forward together to make the journey of life full of love, joy and peace.

In some communities that are labelled as "black" and occupied by people who are poor, the streets are full of adults who are alive until they die, meaning they are broken to the point where they are alive for the sake of waiting for the point of death. To them, helping others has only meant sharing burdens and devising means to live to see another day. Petty crime rises in the face of this mind set, where people are trying to survive only minute moments of life instead of being bigger and better, to leave significant marks on the universe. Bad behaviour became permissible, as long as the end justifies the means. In these places, the past and its dark mark dim any hope or light that exists. This is the place where we need to tell people that God is the healer and the provider. In this place we pray for the filling of the Holy Spirit, Who is a teacher and a counsellor.

So, be intentionally helpful. Be a light. Shine brighter and higher than any clouds that surround your people.

Do you want to know that you are living life in the will of God? The way to know that you are is when at least one person says that they look up to you, when at least one person depends on your input, when your gift and talent is being beneficial to someone other than yourself. Be intentionally helpful. Reach out and show someone else the way.

The bible says, in Proverbs 22:9:

> *⁹He who has a generous eye will be blessed,*
> *For he gives of his bread to the poor.*

Do not be dissuaded by people who function and exist to maintain the state of their struggle and who have resisted the process of healing that is available to all of us when we come to Jesus. When you help others you are not wasting your time, your money or your efforts. If we profess to be children of God, we have to have the Spirit of God who gave us His Son. He loved us so much that He gave us His Son Jesus to take up all our problems and troubles so that we can know and have proof that we are loved by God. The same Spirit in us persuades us, as children of God, to help others. The bible says that if we don't we are pretentious about being Christians.

> *¹⁴What does it profit, my brethren, if someone says he has faith but does not have works? Can faith save him? ¹⁵If a brother or a sister is naked and destitute of daily food, ¹⁶and one of you says to them, "Depart in peace, be warmed and filled" but you do not give them the things which are needed for the body, what does it profit? ¹⁷Thus also faith by itself, if it does not have works, is dead.*
>
> JAMES 2: 14-17

Helping others does not only involve giving money away. Teaching someone how to live in the Lord is more important than giving money away. Helping others gain a skill that can sustain them is worthy, as is dedicating your time to a charitable organisation or orphanage, seeking abused women and children, teaching young men how to fear the Lord and so on and so forth. Each and every one of us is a gift, and it is when we come out and help others that we appreciate the masterful work that God has made in creating us.

My dear sister, we are not supposed to live like we are victims and live life under a cloud of pity, as if we are still broken and disempowered. It is the will of God for His Holy Spirit to guide us and fill our journey with joy, peace, love and goodness. We can begin by being helpful as we learn, allowing the knowledge to breed success and in the abundance of success, sharing our gifts and life with others. I pray that you not only survive, but that you live life consciously and intentionally and come to a place where you rest in God's faithfulness and grace.

Let us pray.

> Dear Lord Jesus. Thank You for the gift of life. Thank You for this day, that is beautiful and bright, a new day to start afresh. Where I was carrying the weight of the past, I ask for Your healing; where I was blinded by pain, allow me to see. Prepare me to be used by You so that others may come to know You as I do. This I pray in Your name. Amen.

Today Informs Tomorrow

*I*T IS MY PRAYER AND hope that you have learned from this exhortation what a great gift God gave to us. You were born into a family, in a place that God deemed good for His will in your life. He did not allow you to be born without equipping you with gifts to ensure your growth and maturity. God has all you need and is all you need to come to understand who you are. Your worth is enhanced when you allow God to lead you and order your steps. You have a true reflection of yourself in the universe when you look through God's graceful view. For people who had a mountain of obstacles growing up, when it comes time to make our own choices and to live, it is only by depending on God that we become impactful and become successful. Only God can ignite all the power and strength that He has put in us to enjoy life in abundance on earth.

We have made mistakes and have hurt ourselves and others, but we know God who forgives us and teaches us to forgive ourselves and others. We have come to fully appreciate and love ourselves for who and what we are because the greatest love is God Himself. That love leads us to purpose and purpose connects us to a profitable life from which others can benefit. This is what the pages of this exhortation were intended to spell out. To bring you to a place that is set aside for you. You are so highly esteemed by God the Father that He says in His Word:

> ⁶"What is man that you are mindful of him,
> Or the son of man that You take care of him?
> ⁷You have made him a little lower than the angels;
> You have crowned him with glory and honour,
> And set him over the works of Your hands.
> ⁸You have put all things in subjection under his feet"
> For in that he put all in subjection under him, he left nothing that is not under him. But now we do not yet see all things put under him. ⁹But we see Jesus, who was made a little lower than the angels, for the suffering of death crowned with glory and honour, that He, by the grace of God, might taste death for everyone.
>
> HEBREWS 2: 6-9

My dear sister, you are favoured by the Lord. God designed a position for us to be placed a little lower than angels. We were placed that all things are subject to us to rule over and to subdue for a fulfilling life. That is our heavenly right. We are born into the world that is full of deceit, hatred and darkness. The bible says that there is a ruler in this realm of earth who is a father of lies and a deceiver from whom all deceit springs. This ruler of earth aims to separate us from God Almighty Who gave us Jesus. God gave us Jesus so that, in the face of worldly temptations, trials and tribulations, we can look upon Jesus and know that He continues to stand on our behalf to lead us to live lives that honour and glorify God.

When Jesus was praying to God for His disciples – and, by extension, the same prayer is prayed for us when we believe in Him and follow Him – He said:

> *[13] But now I come to You, and these things I speak in the world, that they may have My joy fulfilled in themselves. [14] I have given them Your word; and the world has hated them because they are not of the world, just as I am not of the world. [15] I do not pray that You should take them out of the world, but that You should keep them from the evil one. [16] They are not of the world, just as I am not of the world. [17] Sanctify them by Your truth. Your word is truth.*

We are in the world where God has set us up to rule and subdue. Yet the world is full of its own agendas, some of which are pure and obvious evil while others are masked and deceptively passed as being good. The words of this exhortation are to impress on you that we are of God, my dear sister. Everything we are, everything we think, wish and hope for, everything we are becoming is in God. We are here in a world that was created by God for His good pleasure, yet deceivers have come out into the world to bring such calamity that we get lost trying to find ourselves in the world. But we are not lost; we are in the arms of God Almighty.

In the prayer, Jesus says that the world, including those deceivers and those that have been injured and are refusing healing, will hate you when you decide to look at Jesus. They will not like it when you decide to walk in the fullness of His glory and honour Him. They will not like it and they will try to pull you down when you are transformed by the truth. There are other concepts, theories and followings out there; but the Word of God is true. Jesus prays that you will be changed, and filled with this truth, that even when you are in the world, you rise and stand above the common beliefs and live a life that honours Him.

When you understand this, and know that your life has to be lived in the fear of the Lord, loving Him and respecting Him, then you obey Him as our Father who is in heaven. When we obey God, we don't ever get lost, we don't ever hurt ourselves, we don't ever live in fear and doubt as though we are uncertain of what tomorrow holds for us. When we obey God today, He determines and informs our tomorrow to be in Him, in His goodness and in His Grace for the glory of His name.

fear versus Faith

fear is born when we picture death in different forms. All forms of fear, when expressed fully, end in the death of something or someone. *fear* would have you confined and trapped with inability to take the next step. *fear* further says the next step is harmful and will lead to the cancellation of the present in its existing form. *fear* nullifies our faith in God and influences us to make decisions based on what we know and not on what God says.

As a young lady, most of the time fear will cause you to compromise your values and virtue while it threatens you that your future depends on what you see and what is commonly done and not what God says.

When you know who, what and why you are in the Lord, you also know that, when you are obedient to God today, even though fear might say, walk and act according to the standards of the world, FAITH will rise and cause you to stay obedient and true to His word. You know that the faith you have today is able to access and inform a tomorrow you do not yet see.

There are a lot of things that are masked as good and, even when you have learned that they are not the truth of the Word of God, you begin to doubt as to whether they are open to interpretation, as the deceiver will have us believe. The word of God is eternal and does not change.

doubt versus KNOWLEDGE

doubt fully expressed will deceive you into a sense that you live in a vacuum; that there is no real correct way and that there is no clear margin to what is good and what is bad. It gives ways to sin by bringing confusion when it is time to take a stand, and it will have you feeling like you are not good enough to expect more out of life. doubt paints your present situation to be more acceptable and safer than anywhere you can be, no matter how hard you try, unless you employ only methods that doubt will have you follow. Living in a comfort zone, and feeling pressure to go with the masses, and choosing what is done commonly is a language spoken by doubt.

Being a young Christian in this era, you need more than ever not to doubt the ways of God. You need more than ever to trust when He says He knows the end of all things, and that includes how your immediate plans play out and how your life should shape up. God gives us good and perfects gifts. We do not need any alternative ways to behave and any alternative measures to take to reach success. What the Almighty God says in His word is true: there should never be any doubts in our spirits to do His will and to follow His ways. When we make plans for our lives, the first thing to do should always be to seek His guidance, and when our plans are founded in Him and according to His Word, we are guaranteed joy and providence.

Isaiah 55: 6-12 exhorts us to know that today spent in the Lord, informs tomorrow in His presence.

> *⁶Seek the Lord while He may be found,*
> *Call upon Him while He is near.*
> *⁷Let the wicked forsake his way,*
> *And the unrighteous man his thoughts;*
> *Let him return to the Lord,*
> *And He will have mercy on him;*
> *And to our God,*
> *For He will abundantly pardon.*
> *⁸"For my thoughts are not your thoughts,*
> *Nor are your ways My ways," says the Lord.*
> *⁹"For as the heavens are higher than the earth,*
> *So are my thoughts than your thoughts.*
> *¹⁰"For as the rain comes down, and the snow from heaven,*
> *And do not return there,*
> *But water the earth,*
> *And make it bring forth and bud,*
> *That it may give seed to the sower*
> *And bread to the eater,*
> *¹¹So shall My word be that goes forth from my mouth;*

It shall not return to Me void,
But it shall prosper in the thing for which I sent it.
[12]"For you shall go out with joy,
And be led out with peace;
The mountains and the hills
Shall break forth into singing before you,
And all the trees of the field shall clap their hands.

My dear sister, my prayer remains that you live a life full of joy and peace in Jesus; that you are not ever ashamed to choose Him, believe in Him and trust Him. I pray that when the world pushes hard on you, you are able to take a page from all that the women in my generation have done by grace. Make sure to avoid the mistakes we made that hurt both you and ourselves, draw strength from the knowledge that if we were able to make it so can you. Know that when it gets dark and hard, you will look at us and see that our faces have not only changed because of hardship, and you will realise and appreciate the lines that laughter has drawn as we bask in the goodness of the Lord who has remained faithful. Our history is our legacy, our knowledge is your inheritance, but above all know this:

Find favour and high esteem in the sight of God and man.
⁵Trust in the Lord with all your heart,
And lean not on your own understanding;
⁶In all your ways acknowledge Him,
And he shall direct your paths.
⁷Do not be wise in your own eyes;
Fear the Lord and depart from evil.
⁸It will be health to your flesh,
And strength to your bones.

PROVERBS 3: 4 – 8

I pray for the blessings of our Lord Jesus Christ upon you and those you reach.
    Amen

Now to God be the glory. Amen

www.ingramcontent.com/pod-product-compliance
Lightning Source LLC
Chambersburg PA
CBHW051754040426
42446CB00007B/366

9 780620 813990